T0123223

MACAT

An Analysis of

Toni Morrison's

Playing in the Dark: Whiteness and the Literary Imagination

Karina Jakubowicz
with
Adam Perchard

Published by Macat International Ltd
24:13 Coda Centre, 189 Munster Road, London SW6 6AW.

Distributed exclusively by Routledge
2 Park Square, Milton Park, Abingdon, Oxon OX14 4RN
711 Third Avenue, New York, NY 10017, USA

Routledge is an imprint of the Taylor & Francis Group, an informa business

www.macat.com
info@macat.com

Cataloguing in Publication Data
A catalogue record for this book is available from the British Library.
Library of Congress Cataloguing-in-Publication Data is available upon request.
Cover illustration: Kim Thompson

ISBN 978-1-912302-88-8 (hardback)
ISBN 978-1-912128-91-4 (paperback)
ISBN 978-1-912281-76-3 (e-book)

Notice
The information in this book is designed to orientate readers of the work under analysis,
to elucidate and contextualise its key ideas and themes, and to aid in the development
of critical thinking skills. It is not meant to be used, nor should it be used, as a
substitute for original thinking or in place of original writing or research. References and
notes are provided for informational purposes and their presence does not constitute
endorsement of the information or opinions therein. This book is presented solely for
educational purposes. It is sold on the understanding that the publisher is not engaged
to provide any scholarly advice. The publisher has made every effort to ensure that
this book is accurate and up-to-date, but makes no warranties or representations with
regard to the completeness or reliability of the information it contains. The information
and the opinions provided herein are not guaranteed or warranted to produce particular
results and may not be suitable for students of every ability. The publisher shall not be
liable for any loss, damage or disruption arising from any errors or omissions, or from
the use of this book, including, but not limited to, special, incidental, consequential or
other damages caused, or alleged to have been caused, directly or indirectly, by the
information contained within.

CONTENTS

WAYS IN TO THE TEXT

Who Is Toni Morrison?   9

What Does *Playing in the Dark* Say?   10

Why Does *Playing in the Dark* Matter?   12

SECTION 1: INFLUENCES

Module 1: The Author and the Historical Context   15

Module 2: Academic Context   20

Module 3: The Problem   24

Module 4: The Author's Contribution   29

SECTION 2: IDEAS

Module 5: Main Ideas   36

Module 6: Secondary Ideas   41

Module 7: Achievement   46

Module 8: Place in the Author's Work   50

SECTION 3: IMPACT

Module 9: The First Responses   55

Module 10: The Evolving Debate   60

Module 11: Impact and Influence Today   65

Module 12: Where Next?   70

Glossary of Terms   75

People Mentioned in the Text   80

Works Cited   86

THE MACAT LIBRARY

The Macat Library is a series of unique academic explorations of seminal works in the humanities and social sciences – books and papers that have had a significant and widely recognised impact on their disciplines. It has been created to serve as much more than just a summary of what lies between the covers of a great book. It illuminates and explores the influences on, ideas of, and impact of that book. Our goal is to offer a learning resource that encourages critical thinking and fosters a better, deeper understanding of important ideas.

Each publication is divided into three Sections: Influences, Ideas, and Impact. Each Section has four Modules. These explore every important facet of the work, and the responses to it.

This Section-Module structure makes a Macat Library book easy to use, but it has another important feature. Because each Macat book is written to the same format, it is possible (and encouraged!) to cross-reference multiple Macat books along the same lines of inquiry or research. This allows the reader to open up interesting interdisciplinary pathways.

To further aid your reading, lists of glossary terms and people mentioned are included at the end of this book (these are indicated by an asterisk [*] throughout) – as well as a list of works cited.

Macat has worked with the University of Cambridge to identify the elements of critical thinking and understand the ways in which six different skills combine to enable effective thinking.
Three allow us to fully understand a problem; three more give us the tools to solve it. Together, these six skills make up the **PACIER** model of critical thinking. They are:

ANALYSIS – understanding how an argument is built
EVALUATION – exploring the strengths and weaknesses of an argument
INTERPRETATION – understanding issues of meaning

CREATIVE THINKING – coming up with new ideas and fresh connections
PROBLEM-SOLVING – producing strong solutions
REASONING – creating strong arguments

To find out more, visit **WWW.MACAT.COM.**

CRITICAL THINKING AND *PLAYING IN THE DARK*

Primary critical thinking skill: INTERPRETATION
Secondary critical thinking skill: CREATIVE THINKING

Toni Morrison's *Playing in the Dark: Whiteness and the Literary Imagination* is a seminal piece of literary criticism, and a masterclass in the critical thinking skill of interpretation.

Interpretation plays a vital role in critical thinking: it focuses on interrogating accepted meanings and laying down clear definitions on which a strong argument can be built. Both history and literary history in the US have frequently revolved around understanding how Americans define themselves and each other, and Morrison's work seeks to investigate, question, and redefine one of the central concepts in American history and American literary history: color.. Morrison turned to the classics of American literature to ask how authors had chosen to define the terms 'black' and 'white.' Instead of accepting traditional interpretations of these works, Morrison examined the way in which 'whiteness' defines itself through 'blackness,' and vice versa. Black bondage and the myths of black inferiority and savagery, she showed, allowed white America to indulge its own defining myths – viewing itself as free, civilized, and innocent.

A classic of subtle and incisive interpretation, *Playing in the Dark* shows just how crucial and how complex simple-looking definitions can be.

ABOUT THE AUTHOR OF THE ORIGINAL WORK

Toni Morrison is one of America's most respected living authors. She was born into a working-class family in Ohio in 1931. Her parents had migrated to the North, hoping to escape the harsh racial segregation of the Southern states, and grew up listening to the African American folktales they brought with them. An author and esteemed public intellectual, Morrison is best known for her 11 novels, as well as for her insightful literary criticism. Her work has earned her numerous prestigious honors, including the Pulitzer Prize and the American Book Award. In 1993 Morrison became the first black woman to be awarded the Nobel Prize in literature.

ABOUT THE AUTHOR OF THE ANALYSIS

Karina Jakubowicz is a doctoral student in English literature at University College, London.

Adam Perchard took his PhD in post-colonial literature at the University of York. He has been awarded research fellowships by Emory University, Atlanta, the Indian National Trust for Arts and Cultural Heritage, and the University of York, and currently teaches at Queen Mary, University of London. Dr Perchard's current research focuses on disputing the discourses of cultural incommensurability emblematised and catalysed by the Rushdie Affair.

ABOUT MACAT

GREAT WORKS FOR CRITICAL THINKING

Macat is focused on making the ideas of the world's great thinkers accessible and comprehensible to everybody, everywhere, in ways that promote the development of enhanced critical thinking skills.

It works with leading academics from the world's top universities to produce new analyses that focus on the ideas and the impact of the most influential works ever written across a wide variety of academic disciplines. Each of the works that sit at the heart of its growing library is an enduring example of great thinking. But by setting them in context – and looking at the influences that shaped their authors, as well as the responses they provoked – Macat encourages readers to look at these classics and game-changers with fresh eyes. Readers learn to think, engage and challenge their ideas, rather than simply accepting them.

'Macat offers an amazing first-of-its-kind tool for interdisciplinary learning and research. Its focus on works that transformed their disciplines and its rigorous approach, drawing on the world's leading experts and educational institutions, opens up a world-class education to anyone.'

Andreas Schleicher,
Director for Education and Skills, Organisation for Economic
Co-operation and Development

'Macat is taking on some of the major challenges in university education … They have drawn together a strong team of active academics who are producing teaching materials that are novel in the breadth of their approach.'

Prof Lord Broers,
former Vice-Chancellor of the University of Cambridge

'The Macat vision is exceptionally exciting. It focuses upon new modes of learning which analyse and explain seminal texts which have profoundly influenced world thinking and so social and economic development. It promotes the kind of critical thinking which is essential for any society and economy.
This is the learning of the future.'

Rt Hon Charles Clarke, former UK Secretary of State for Education

'The Macat analyses provide immediate access to the critical conversation surrounding the books that have shaped their respective discipline, which will make them an invaluable resource to all of those, students and teachers, working in the field.'

Professor William Tronzo, University of California at San Diego

WAYS IN TO THE TEXT

KEY POINTS

- Toni Morrison is a Nobel Prize–winning African American author and literary critic. She is often considered America's greatest living novelist.

- *Playing in the Dark* argues that the representation of African Americans in literature has shaped American national identity.

- Instead of studying race only in terms of oppressed minorities, Morrison investigates the formation of "whiteness" in opposition to social constructs of "blackness."

Who is Toni Morrison?

Toni Morrison, the author of *Playing in the Dark: Whiteness and the Literary Imagination* (1992), is one of the best-loved, best-selling, and most highly decorated living authors in the United States. She was born to a working-class family in Ohio in 1931, a time of economic depression and stark racial tension. Morrison always excelled academically, earning her bachelor's degree at Howard University* and her master's at Cornell University;* these achievements set the foundation for her current status as one of the country's most well-respected public intellectuals.

In the 1970s she worked as an editor in New York, where she used her position to champion the work of many black writers. She went on to write 11 novels, winning (among other accolades) the Pulitzer Prize for fiction* and the American Book Award* for *Beloved* in 1988, and the Nobel Prize in literature* in 1993. An esteemed scholar in addition to being a novelist, Morrison has held professorships at prestigious universities, including Harvard* and Princeton.*

Although she never formally aligned herself with any specific political organizations of the 1960s and 1970s, such as the American Civil Rights Movement* (the term for the various mid-twentieth-century social movements founded on the desire to secure equal rights for all Americans) or the Black Arts Movement* (a cultural movement with influence in the spheres of theatre, literature, and music), her novels and non-fiction work have always been driven by an awareness of racial injustice and a desire to undermine it. In addition to her novels and works of literary criticism, Morrison has also written plays, children's books, and even an opera libretto.

What Does *Playing in the Dark* Say?

Playing in the Dark engages with race in its social aspects—as a system where quality judgments are made, degrees of oppression are imposed, or privilege is granted on the basis of skin color. Morrison argues that over hundreds of years, layers of associations such as repulsion, desire, and fear have been projected onto African Americans. But rather than simply defining the racist conception of black Americans, Morrison proposes that these ideas of blackness actually serve as a foil against which white America defines itself.

For Morrison, discussions of race traditionally tend to focus only on people who suffer under racial hierarchies; although the idea of whiteness is just as important, she says, it is almost always taken for granted. Looking closely at representations of race in literature, regardless of whether the work intentionally deals with issues of race or racism, provides a rich and relevant way to understand the complex power dynamics of present-day America. The convention of ignoring race in order to appear polite is, Morrison asserts, actually preventing the open discussion that is necessary to address and eventually eradicate racism.

As she analyzes texts by a range of seminal, or groundbreaking, American authors from the nineteenth and twentieth centuries, Morrison shows that African Americans are not only an important presence in classic American literature, they actually define it. While European colonial nations such as Britain, Spain, and France were formed long before the trade in African slaves began, slavery was a central part of nation-building in the United States. As the American national identity began to consolidate as a concept, free white settlers were able to unify through a shared idea of *what they were not*—namely, enslaved black people. Whether they were originally from Britain or Holland, France or Spain, white settlers in America were able to form a coherent group—a nation—because they were, eventually, brought together by an idea of white identity.

This idea relied on the construction of the idea of blackness or, as Morrison calls it, Africanism.*

While there are many texts that directly represent black people as inferior to white people, Morrison argues that racial dynamics in American literature are more complicated than that. White writers also project feelings of desire and love onto African Americans in literature at the same time as they project feelings such as dread, fear, and contempt. Blackness, in the American literary imagination, is bound up with ideas of the unknown, the irrational, and the primitive, while whiteness is associated with knowledge, reason, and civilization. Morrison writes that these ideas are all at the heart of the genre of the Gothic* romance*—a literary form often concerned with the supernatural and the evocation of feelings of desire and fear—in American literature. For Morrison, this genre is closely linked to the most central pillar of American national identity: the American

Dream* (the notion that, with application, all citizens are capable of achieving status and prosperity).

Why Does *Playing in the Dark* Matter?

Toni Morrison's *Playing in the Dark* has had a profound impact on the study of literature and on the attitudes towards African American culture and history within academia. One critic called it a "brilliant and provocative book" that "no critic of American culture [could] afford to ignore."[1] Another claims that "it is hard not to look back on [the year that *Playing in the Dark* was published] as a watershed moment in American letters."[2] *Playing in the Dark* helped to bring about a significant reshaping of attitudes to race in the humanities, and encouraged the consideration of African American experience in an academic context.

Playing in the Dark has become a key text in disciplines across the humanities. Morrison's rethinking of the representation of race and the role it plays in creating national identity has been applied to feminism* (a set of political and intellectual currents founded on the desire to achieve equality between the sexes), queer theory* (an avenue of inquiry into issues of gender, identity, and sexualities outside what are understood to be social "norms"), history, and postcolonialism* (investigations into the various cultural legacies of colonialism).

Engaging with Morrison's approach not only opens up new avenues of thought for students and introduces the building blocks of contemporary race studies, but also provides a new and valuable set of critical tools. Morrison's method of reading racial dynamics between the lines of American literature is now being used by scholars to unpack the complexities of many other forms of oppression, including religious discrimination, sexism, homophobia,* and socioeconomic inequalities.

At a time when racial tensions in the United States have returned to the forefront of the popular consciousness, with mass protest movements such as Black Lives Matter campaigning against widespread police violence against African Americans, *Playing in the Dark* has perhaps never been so relevant. Beyond the benefits that this text offers scholars of the humanities, it presents valuable opportunities to readers inside and outside the academic world for understanding prejudice, and the ways in which power relations shape social dynamics. As gay people struggle to gain equal rights, as women continue to battle for legal and economic equality, and as people all over the world continue to die in conflicts over religion, the insights Morrison gives us into the way prejudice is formed and practiced, consciously and unconsciously, are as valuable now as they were in 1992. *Playing in the Dark* is one of the most original and important discussions of race, history, and national identity of the twentieth century.

NOTES

1 Shelley Fisher Fishkin, "*Playing in the Dark: Whiteness and the Literary Imagination*. By Toni Morrison," *Journal of American History* 80, no. 2 (1993): 629.

2 Susan Searls Giroux, "Playing in the Dark: Racial Repression and the New Campus Crusade for Diversity," *College Literature* 33, no. 4 (2006): 95.

SECTION 1
INFLUENCES

MODULE 1
THE AUTHOR AND THE HISTORICAL CONTEXT

KEY POINTS

- Toni Morrison's *Playing in the Dark* continues to shape the way issues of race are discussed in many disciplines across the humanities.

- Morrison grew up in a working-class family in Ohio, against a backdrop of racial injustice and her family's memories of generations of oppression.

- One of America's greatest living authors, Morrison's literary criticism is shaped and informed by her experiences as a writer of fiction.

Why Read this Text?

When Toni Morrison's *Playing in the Dark* was published in 1992, it demanded that scholars reassess the role played by African Americans in the formation of American national identity. Now, over 20 years later, it continues to provoke its readers—academics and non-specialists alike—to rethink the status quo (that is, the existing state of affairs).

Morrison asks the reader to consider basic principles such as freedom, equality, and democracy against the bondage, repression, and political disempowerment suffered by African Americans in law and custom in order to bring about a sufficiently sophisticated understanding of persistent racial inequalities. It is not enough to think about race and the history of race relations solely in terms of the minority black community and the creation of often repressive stereotypes within the popular imagination. We must also consider the creation of an idea of whiteness and how its normative* status is

> ❝ Until very recently, and regardless of the race of the author, the readers of virtually all of American fiction have been positioned as white. I am interested to know what that assumption has meant to the literary imagination ... In other words, how is 'literary whiteness' and 'literary blackness' made, and what is the consequence of that construction? ❞
>
> Toni Morrison, *Playing in the Dark: Whiteness and the Literary Imagination*

maintained, that is, the idea of whiteness as the ideal state.

To this end, Morrison develops an idea of Africanism,* a concept that amounts to more than a description of skin color or ethnic background. Instead, it encompasses the many layers of (usually negative, demeaning, or patronizing) associations piled onto black people over the centuries, which allows white America to define itself as the opposite of these characteristics. One of the most important aspects of the text is the process of reading Africanism back into literary texts that might not initially seem to be concerned with race. This critical maneuver has since been taken up by scholars working across a range of disciplines.

Author's Life

Toni Morrison is an African American writer and academic. She was born in Lorain, Ohio in 1931 to a working-class family. Although Lorain was an ethnically mixed town, it was by no means free of the racial oppression that was far more pronounced in the Southern states from which her parents had migrated. In 1949 she attended Howard University,* where she began writing fiction—notably a short story about an African American girl who wished for blue eyes, which later formed the basis for her debut novel *The Bluest Eye* (1970).

She graduated in 1953 with a BA in English (with a minor in

Classics), and went on to complete a master's degree in English at Cornell University* in 1955. She returned to Howard to work as an instructor in English between 1957 and 1964, a period during which she married the architect Harold Morrison,* had two sons with him, and divorced him. *Playing in the Dark* was partly informed by Morrison's experience as a professor, and she credited the academic environment with allowing her to advance her research and "test ideas with exceptional students."[1] She felt so indebted to these students for their input that she dedicated the book to several of them.

Her literary career began with the publication of *The Bluest Eye* in 1970, and in 1981 she was elected to the American Academy of Arts and Letters.* In 1988 she won the Pulitzer Prize for fiction;* in 1993 she became the first woman of color to be awarded the Nobel Prize in literature;* and in 2012 she received the Presidential Medal of Freedom,* the highest civilian honor bestowed in the United States.

Author's Background

Morrison grew up in an underprivileged, racially mixed town in Ohio in the 1930s. Suffering the double privations of poverty and racial prejudice, her parents and grandparents (who had migrated from the South) often discussed the injustice of slavery and legally enforced segregation, but also passed down a rich body of Southern African American folklore. By the time Morrison reached adulthood, the active opposition to racial segregation and other forms of oppression had developed into the Civil Rights Movement.* Although Morrison never played an active role in this movement, her interest in the political, social, and artistic ramifications of race continued to grow during her professional life. While also teaching at universities, she became an editor, and promoted the work of many black authors in her position at the prestigious publishing company Random House* in the 1970s and 1980s.

Though she was never formally a part of the Black Arts

Movement* (a 1960s and 1970s movement in literature, theatre, dance, and music), Morrison's focus on championing black writers in the publishing industry, and her own writing—which expressed many contemporary and historical realities of African American life—were very much in line with what the Black Arts stood for. Similarly, while reluctant to pigeonhole herself as a feminist,* she recognized an ideological connection between racism and the oppression of women, and this link is one of the characteristic features of second-wave feminism* (the strand of feminist activism that began in the 1960s and that saw cultural and political inequalities as inextricably linked).

Her work draws on the advances made by many African American scholars, most notably W. E. B. Du Bois,* a historian and sociologist* (that is, a scholar of the functioning of human society) whose pioneering work in the first half of the twentieth century insisted that the social realities of black history and contemporary life should be studied, and demanded equal access to education as an urgent social imperative. This focus on the university as a battleground in the fight for racial equality is something Morrison continues in *Playing in the Dark*. The literary critic and scholar Henry Louis Gates, Jr.,* writing from the 1980s onwards, is another powerful voice in this struggle. Like Morrison, his work encompasses cultural criticism as well as a number of edited works documenting black history, and he occupies a similar niche in American culture as an outspoken and highly regarded public intellectual.

Morrison's dissatisfaction with academic attitudes to race in literature was partly what shaped the arguments she outlines in *Playing in the Dark*. She observes that many academics ignore racial difference in a bid to appear politically correct; "the habit of ignoring race," she writes, "is understood to be a graceful, even generous, liberal gesture. To notice is to recognize an already discredited difference."[2] In Morrison's view, pretending not to notice race may protect an individual from coming across as racist, but inhibits open, productive discussion of a serious social issue. *Playing in the Dark* is a direct challenge to this ultimately counterproductive convention.

NOTES

1   Toni Morrison, dedication in *Playing in the Dark: Whiteness and the Literary Imagination* (New York: Vintage Books, 1993).

2   Morrison, *Playing in the Dark*, 9–10.

MODULE 2
ACADEMIC CONTEXT

KEY POINTS

- Toni Morrison is both an influential literary critic and an author at the pinnacle of her field, and these two roles overlap in her work.

- *Playing in the Dark* is a major call to arms for literary critics to begin thinking about the construction of whiteness in the American national identity.

- Morrison has sometimes been criticized for failing to give adequate credit to earlier scholars whose work on race in literature paved the way for *Playing in the Dark*.

The Work In Its Context

Toni Morrison published *Playing in the Dark: Whiteness and the Literary Imagination* in the midst of what are now known as the Culture Wars*—a fiery debate within American universities about whether literary studies should reduce the dominance of traditional, canonical texts (mostly by white male authors) to make room for the examination of work from more marginalized groups, such as non-white and female authors. Morrison's intervention into this dispute was timely, but many commentators noted the lack of references in *Playing in the Dark* to previous critiques of race in literature.

African American criticism was well established by the early 1990s. Thinkers from the cultural movement of 1919 to 1937 known as the Harlem Renaissance* had been revisited in light of the Black Arts Movement* of the 1960s and 1970s and the Civil Rights Movement* of the 1950s and 1960s to highlight the political and cultural inequalities facing African Americans. Not only had the sociologist* W. E. B. Du Bois* and, later, the literary critic Henry Louis Gates, Jr.*

> ❝ Toni Morrison's analyses in *Playing in the Dark* expand upon Du Bois's meditation in *Souls [The Souls of Black Folk]* to suggest that in the world of critical exegesis [i.e. interpretation] of canonical* American literature, there can be no true literary self-consciousness in American letters as long as such critical analyses continue to believe that canonical American literature is uninformed and unshaped by the presence of, first, Africans and then African Americans in the United States. ❞
>
> Glyne Griffith, "Reading in the Dark: Race, Literature, and the Discourse of Blackness"

written foundational texts in African American literary criticism* decades before,[1] but by the time *Playing in the Dark* was written, postcolonial studies* had established a significant presence in the world of academia. As a multidisciplinary movement aimed at revealing the violent histories and destructive legacies of colonialism, postcolonialism shares many of Morrison's concerns; indeed, she later admitted that *Playing in the Dark* was indebted to the Palestinian American theorist Edward Said's* seminal work *Orientalism* (1978).

Overview of the Field

One flaw in early African American literary criticism—a school of literary studies that reads American literature in the light of African American history, culture, and experience—is that it had typically focused only on the representation of African Americans and on the work of African American artists. Morrison's approach differed in that it emphasized the representation of both races, and demonstrated how each was used to define the other. As she writes, "the scholarship that looks into the mind, imagination, and behavior of slaves is valuable.

But equally valuable is a serious intellectual effort to see what racial ideology does to the mind, imagination, and behavior of masters."[2]

Another unique aspect of Morrison's work is her attempt to focus on concepts of "whiteness" or "blackness" instead of purely on black writers and characters while taking whiteness for granted in discussions about race. She describes her work as "an investigation into the ways in which a nonwhite Africanlike (or Africanist)* presence or persona was constructed in the United States and the imaginative uses this fabricated presence served."[3] By exploring signifiers of blackness—those things that act as signs indicating what is understood to be black identity—and by arguing that these are pervasive throughout American literature, Morrison is able to find an Africanist presence even in those novels that do not have African American characters.

Academic Influences

Morrison was influenced not only by the work of scholars such as Du Bois and Gates in the field of African American literary criticism, and Edward Said in postcolonialism, but also by the work of black feminists such as Barbara Smith,* who first opened up the discussion of the overlapping oppressions of racism and sexism. Morrison's ideas about the formation of knowledge and about knowledge as a means of constructing and maintaining unjust social structures owe a great deal to French theorists of the 1970s and 1980s, in particular the philosopher and cultural historian Michel Foucault.*

Playing in the Dark is one of the few texts that Morrison wrote with an academic audience in mind. It was written when Morrison was teaching at Harvard* and Princeton,* two of the most prestigious seats of learning in the United States, and was shaped by the discussions that she was having with her students at the time.

Morrison observed that her students had been taught implicitly to read American literature as though it was devoid of African American influence, and she attempted to place the supposedly peripheral subject of race at the core of their literary understanding. This, perhaps, makes it all the more surprising that Morrison included so little about existing scholarship on African Americans and literature in her text. It seems likely that this was because *Playing in the Dark* was adapted from a series of lectures, and therefore Morrison wanted to keep the tone conversational, and not bogged down by too many academic references.

Although the text was intended primarily for an academic audience, its approachable, poetic language and Morrison's increasing fame meant the book reached a much wider audience. When *Playing in the Dark* was published she was one year away from winning the Nobel Prize in literature.*

NOTES

1   See W. E. B. Du Bois, *The Souls of Black Folk* (Chicago: A. C. McClurg, 1903); Henry Louis Gates, Jr., *Figures in Black: Words, Signs, and the "Racial" Self* (New York: Oxford University Press, 1987), among many others.

2   Toni Morrison, *Playing in the Dark: Whiteness and the Literary Imagination* (New York: Vintage Books, 1993), 11–12.

3   Morrison, *Playing in the Dark*, 6.

MODULE 3
THE PROBLEM

KEY POINTS

- Toni Morrison was writing at a time when the Culture Wars* were raging in American universities. This was a fierce debate about whether the traditional literary canon* should be expanded to include work by female writers and authors from racial minorities.

- Thinkers such as the historian and social critic Arthur M. Schlesinger, Jr.* argued that an excessive emphasis on racial identity could endanger the unity of American society.

- Morrison argued that it was impossible to consider American society *without* thinking about race.

Core Question

At the heart of Toni Morrison's book *Playing in the Dark* is the question of how concepts of racial blackness and whiteness are constructed in literature and society. She defines her work as "an investigation into the ways in which a nonwhite, Africanlike (or Africanist)* presence or persona was constructed in the United States, and the imaginative uses this fabricated presence served."[1]

This investigation sheds light on inconsistencies in practice within American values, such as the contradiction between the principle of personal liberty as the nation's defining virtue and the use of slave labor to build that nation. For Morrison, it is the presence of an enslaved population that allowed white America to define itself as fundamentally free. When she writes about an Africanist presence, Morrison is saying that the idea of blackness is not just about skin color or the many limiting ideas connected to black skin in the minds

> ❝ As for the culture, the imaginative and historical terrain upon which early American writers journeyed is in large measure shaped by the presence of the racial other. Statements to the contrary, insisting on the meaninglessness of race to the American identity, are themselves full of meaning. The world does not become raceless or will not become unracialized by assertion. ❞
>
> Toni Morrison, *Playing in the Dark: Whiteness and the Literary Imagination*

of European Americans. Instead, it is a broad, complex culture of thought about black people that shapes the way both black people and white people think about themselves. Africanism is also a metaphor for anxieties about sex, violence, and the unknown in American culture and a vehicle for expressing the deep-seated fears underpinning American society.

Morrison's inquiry is as political as it is literary since she believes that literature both informs and is informed by society. Morrison claims her inquiry rises out of what she knows about the ways that writers can turn elements of their social background into aspects of language—"the ways they tell their stories, fight secret wars, limn out [i.e. lay out] all sorts of debates blanketed in their text."[2] In other words, Morrison is aware that when writers write they create a world of discussions beneath the surface level of the text and that a great deal of social commentary takes place between the lines of literature. Morrison feels that by exploring the presence of race in American literature, she is also exposing the importance of race in American history and in constructed ideas of American identity.

The Participants

The social critic Arthur M. Schlesinger, Jr.'s *The Disuniting of America: Reflections on a Multicultural Society*, published the same year as *Playing* *in the Dark*, is one of a raft of publications written in the early 1990s warning that projects such as Morrison's, which emphasized social and racial difference, stood to endanger the unity of American society. The conflict between thinkers who believed that American culture needed to be opened up to consider the cultural contributions of minorities, and those who believed that the core, Eurocentric values of American culture had to be maintained, came to be called the Culture Wars. As Andrew Hartman explains, "the culture wars rose out of the 1960s. They are specific to the 1980s and 1990s, when national debates about what it means to be an American took on added emphasis, meaning and anger as a result of the social movements of the 1960s. We're talking about Civil Rights, the Black Power Movement*..."[3]

Although politically conscious, Morrison had not played an active role in earlier political movements as she found it difficult to align her views neatly with any one campaign. She writes: "I was not in favor of integration. But I couldn't officially say that, because I knew the terror and the abuses of segregation. But integration also meant that we would not have a fine black college or fine black education."[4] Segregation, legally mandated by a set of rules known as the Jim Crow Laws,* was the policy of separating black people and white people at schools and universities, as well as on transport and in social spaces such as movie theaters. Integration meant the end of official racial divides, but in opposing it, Morrison is voicing her fears about the end of educational institutions in which black people could learn in an environment free of white discrimination. Such anxieties about government measures to end discrimination in educational institutions without taking into consideration the entrenched cultural and social inequalities that would continue to affect African Americans are at the heart of Morrison's objections to the ideas of thinkers like Schlesinger.

The Contemporary Debate

In *Playing in the Dark*, Toni Morrison is concerned with changing the way that both academics and readers encounter American literature. As she states in the first lines of the text, "these chapters put forth an argument for extending the study of American literature into what I hope will be a wider landscape."[5]

In this project, she was not only defying specific critics such as Harold Bloom*—whose traditionalist views of what should be studied resisted changing the canon to include African American authors—she was also contending with what the US literature scholar Susan Searls Giroux calls "the official colorblinding rhetoric of the Reagan*–Bush* era* with its insistence that 'race no longer matters,' effectively used to silence any serious discussion of everyday racisms, [and] its tendency toward historical denial precluding any connection between past and present inequality."[6] Like Giroux, Morrison believes that color-blindness—intentionally ignoring race—is a way of ignoring rather than solving the problem of racial inequality.

In *Playing in the Dark*, Morrison asserts that the questions of race, and of the history of racial inequality, are central to present-day America. While Schlesinger and other anti-multiculturalists insist that social theory that emphasizes race risks dividing America along racial lines, for Morrison, and for critics such as the African American scholar Barbara Smith,* the American nation is (and has always been) divided along lines of racial inequality and oppression—and this reality needs to be confronted rather than ignored.

NOTES

1   Toni Morrison, *Playing in the Dark: Whiteness and the Literary Imagination* (New York: Vintage Books, 1993), 6.

2   Morrison, *Playing in the Dark*, 4.

3   Micah Uetricht, "The Culture Wars Are Over—And They Are Not Coming Back," *In These Times*, June 11, 2015, accessed September 30, 2015, http://inthesetimes.com/article/18022/culture_wars_andrew_hartman.

4   R. K. Lester, "An Interview With Toni Morrison, Hessian Radio Network, Frankfurt, West Germany," in *Critical Essays on Toni Morrison*, ed. Nellie Y. McKay (Boston: G. K. Hall, 1988), 51.

5   Morrison, *Playing in the Dark*, 3.

6   Susan Searls Giroux, "Playing in the Dark: Racial Repression and the New Campus Crusade for Diversity," *College Literature* 33, no. 4 (2006): 96.

MODULE 4
THE AUTHOR'S CONTRIBUTION

KEY POINTS

- *Playing in the Dark* seeks to restore questions of race to the study of American literature, and to examine the role of whiteness in the formation of American national identity.

- This emphasis on whiteness, rather than solely on the formation of black identity, revolutionized American literary criticism.

- Morrison's work built on African American literary criticism,* postcolonial studies,* and feminism,* as well as on historical calls for equality, such as the Civil Rights Movement* of the 1950s and 1960s.

Author's Aims

Toni Morrison's primary aim in writing *Playing in the Dark: Whiteness and the Literary Imagination* was to argue for the importance of Africanism*—a mode of representing African American people, particularly negatively—in the American literary imagination. She felt that the convention of reading literature as universal or race-free was a missed opportunity. For Morrison, an awareness of race and identity within literature—regardless of whether direct, aggressive racism formed part of the plot or characterization—could provide a sophisticated insight into how racial dominance is formed and maintained off the page.

Subtext* (that is, meaning in a text that must be inferred by the reader) and the unsaid in literature speak volumes, and literature without black characters still carries the specter of race and power inequalities, even if the majority of mainstream literary critics tend to read these works as somehow raceless. In American fiction, the race of

> ❝ It is *the* problem of the writing, to let my imagination have full rein, and for me to be the only one to rein it in … As an African American writer writing about African Americans, can I talk about evil in a certain way without demonizing people who have been traditionally associated in the minds of bigots and racists with evil? I have to claim that, as we all do. Do I have to use skin privileges when I describe people? … Can I give up the inherent power of signaling race? It *has* power. ❞
>
> Toni Morrison, "Loose Magic: A. J. Verdelle Interviews Toni Morrison"

white characters is generally marked by omission: in her discussion of the novelist Ernest Hemingway's* *To Have and Have Not*, for example, Morrison says of one secondary character, "Eddy is white, and we know he is because nobody says so."[1] This convention passively equates whiteness with the universal (or "normal"), and Morrison urges literary critics to acknowledge this as problematic.

"Above all," she writes, "I am interested in how agendas in criticism have disguised themselves and, in so doing, impoverished the literature it studies."[2] In neglecting issues of race, literary criticism not only fails to unlock vital information about the role of race in forming American national identity, it also reinforces the misguided view that America's race problem can be effectively understood through considerations of blackness alone.

By changing attitudes toward race in academic scholarship, Morrison aimed to help the United States at large recognize the power of race to both divide and shape society. It is not just black people whose lives have been shaped by centuries of racism, Morrison insists, and critics must also pay attention to "the impact of racism on those who perpetuate it."[3] She was offering not just a new way of reading literature—searching for the racial dynamics between the lines—but a new way of looking at history.

Morrison effectively anticipates the potential danger that her analysis could be misinterpreted as condemning the work that forms her primary source material, or as a suggestion that this work should no longer be studied. She is careful to note that she is looking at *racial* language rather than racist language, expressing admiration for these writers as she evaluates the Africanist presence in their work. *Playing in the Dark* claims that no one, either in literature departments at universities or in the nation as a whole, can think about themselves or their culture without thinking about race. Morrison aimed to reshape the way America saw itself, and by doing so, she hoped to change the shape of race relations in the future.

Approach

Playing in the Dark first appeared as Toni Morrison's 1992 delivery of the William E. Massey, Sr., Lectures in the History of American Civilization* at Harvard University,* and this origin is evident in the book. Each of the three chapters is equivalent to one of the three lectures. She had arrived at her study of the representation of race in literature through her role as a writer, editor, and scholar of fiction. When Morrison wrote *Playing in the Dark* she was already a Pulitzer Prize–winning[x] author, and it is her experience as a writer that she makes central to her understanding of literary works. This experience of authorship prompted her to consider how free she could be as an "African-American woman writer in [a] genderized, sexualized, wholly racialized world."[4]

For Morrison, a writer's work is not just passively shaped by the dominant ideas and prejudices of her environment. Fiction can also surmount these prejudices through a conscious awareness of the author's own social privilege. *Playing in the Dark* has a sophisticated, dynamic, forward-looking quality that takes literature as more than a way of recording social injustice, instead highlighting its potential to overcome it.

The book's title could be interpreted as echoing elements of Morrison's literary critical approach. While darkness may at first seem like an unlikely setting for "play" to take place in, here again Morrison may be referring to the ambivalent nature of Africanism—something that white America is both afraid of and magnetized toward—and the imaginary location where their anxieties and fears play out. In real life, literally *playing in the dark* would be ill-advised. In this way, the title could be read as a metaphor for writing and reading from a color-blind perspective, suggesting that these activities are going on, in a sense, with our eyes closed to the sociopolitical realities of race that surround us all the time. Would we all be better off if, instead, we *shed light* on the act of creating and consuming literature?

Contribution in Context

In the 1970s and 1980s, a significant number of universities established courses and departments dedicated to the study of underrepresented people, such as African American Studies and Women's Studies, granting overdue recognition to contributions to culture beyond those of white men. *Playing in the Dark* is a vital contribution to the larger project of redefining *what* is worthy of study, and a major innovation in *how* we think about literature, culture, identity, and power. Morrison's ideas do not only complement existing scholarship on African American literary criticism, they are also transferable to postcolonial, feminist, and queer* readings of literature.

Morrison was also very receptive to the burgeoning second-wave feminist movement* of the 1960s to the 1980s, with its particular focus on the need for civic, cultural, and social equality between the sexes. She acknowledged that the conversations concerning African American culture were "… located in the assault that the feminist scholarship of men and women (black and white) made and continues to make on traditional literary discourse. The male part of the white male equation is already deeply engaged, and no one believes the body of literature and its criticism will ever again be what it was."[5]

Here, Morrison is expressing her hope that the way race is read and written in literature will be permanently transformed in the same way that feminist criticism has changed the way gender is treated in literary studies. *Playing in the Dark*, like much of the work being produced by contemporary feminists, built on the work carried out by French theorists such as Michel Foucault* in the 1980s involving studying the relationship between knowledge and power. As with debates concerning gender and power, Morrison's argument is based on the notion that if the powerful members of society have the greatest ability to produce culture, then much of this culture will reinforce the position of those who are powerful. Furthermore, this reinforcing of social power relations (the way that power is expressed in things such as social status) in culture will largely appear "natural," presented through conventions readers easily take for granted. These dynamics are often only visible through the kind of close, between-the-lines reading that Morrison proposes.

Although *Playing in the Dark* contributed to ongoing debates about culture and politics in America, Morrison has never easily associated herself with particular intellectual movements. One critic describes her as "refusing the tradition of protest fiction, refusing to subscribe to some of the tenets of the Black [Arts Movement] of the 1960s, refusing also any easy identification with the women's movement," yet writing works which are "nevertheless decidedly political, aesthetic and feminist."[6]

NOTES

1   Toni Morrison, *Playing in the Dark: Whiteness and the Literary Imagination* (New York: Vintage Books, 1993), 72.

2   Morrison, *Playing in the Dark*, 8.

3   Morrison, *Playing in the Dark*, 11.

4   Morrison, *Playing in the Dark*, 4.

5   Angelyn Mitchell, ed., *Within the Circle: An Anthology of African American Literature* (Durham, NC: Duke University Press, 1994), 368–89.

6   Jill Matus, *Toni Morrison* (Manchester: Manchester University Press, 1998), 13.

SECTION 2
IDEAS

MODULE 5
MAIN IDEAS

KEY POINTS

- *Playing in the Dark* argues that representations of African Americans in American literature have shaped American national identity.

- Morrison's central point is that concepts of whiteness and Americanness are defined through authors' representations of Africanism.

- Morrison approaches American literature not just as a reader and a critic, but also as an author. *Playing in the Dark* is written in unusually rich literary language for a work of criticism, which is perhaps part of the reason for its enduring popularity.

Key Themes

The central argument of Toni Morrison's *Playing in the Dark: Whiteness and the Literary Imagination* is that a constructed African American identity pervades American literature and has shaped an American national identity that privileges whiteness over blackness.

African Americans have been part of America for four hundred years, and their presence had "shaped the body politic, the Constitution, and the entire history of the culture."[1] Morrison proposes that the belief that African Americans played only a peripheral role in American literature is not just misguided, but also constitutes an act of racial violence. Morrison uses the term Africanism to describe the complex ways in which African Americans are represented in the American literary imagination. The word covers both the direct racism of portraying black people as inferior, and also the web of associations—spoken and unspoken—that the mainstream mentality

> ❝ Whiteness has been taken as the universal against which the Other is constructed as different and racialized ... In *Playing in the Dark*, Morrison notes that whiteness is de-raced and universalized in proportion to the degree of racial blackness assigned to the Africanist* presence in a literary text. ❞
>
> Cathy Moses, *Dissenting Fictions: Identity and Resistance in the Contemporary American Novel*

holds about blackness. Africanism is the implied dread of, and desire for, black people that lies between the lines of American literature, and that allows white American identity to define itself against its supposed opposite. Africanism, for Morrison, is a pervasive literary device that American literary critics have persistently failed to address because of a widespread tendency to avoid acknowledging race.

Morrison is aware of the progress made by earlier studies of African American authors and characters, but wants to extend their scope by deconstructing the idea of whiteness as well as that of blackness in relation to race, and the largely unseen ways in which the latter might be said to create the former:

"[T]he scholarship that looks into the mind, imagination, and behavior of slaves is valuable. But equally valuable is a serious intellectual effort to see what racial ideology does to the mind, imagination, and behavior of masters."[2]

Here, Morrison equates the position of the master with that of the white man or woman, who might not be a master in the literal sense, but who has historically derived social privilege from the system of racial inequality. Morrison feels that the literature produced by these "masters" affords an insight into how race affects their own sense of identity, and can be as important in the study of race as those books written by black people.

The literary effects of Africanism mean that black characters in novels work as metaphors for a range of wider social issues and anxieties. They are "a way of referring to and disguising forces, events, classes, and expressions of social decay and economic division far more threatening to the body politic than biological 'race' ever was."[3] This leads to the construction of whiteness as the absence of race, the norm, so leaving African Americans defined by the color of their skin—and by the negative cultural associations projected onto that color.

Exploring the Ideas

Playing in the Dark is made up of three essays. In each, Morrison considers how concepts of whiteness and Americanness are defined through authors' representations of Africanism and asks what role this plays in the writer's imagination. She begins by reacting to what she feels is "a tacit agreement among literary scholars" that American literature has been the preserve of white male views "without relationship to and removed from the overwhelming presence of black people in the United States."[4] Morrison argues that even though books may not appear to concern African Americans, the imagination of the American author is strongly affected by a "carefully observed, and carefully invented, Africanist presence."[5] She goes on to show the impossibility of approaching white identity without considering its relation to blackness through a detailed reading of the novelist Willa Cather's* *Sapphira and the Slave Girl* (1940).[6]

This idea is extended in the second and third essays, "Romancing the Shadow" and "Disturbing Nurses and the Kindness of Sharks." Here, Morrison examines seemingly peripheral African American characters in the work of the poet and short-story writer Edgar Allan Poe* and the Nobel Prize–winning* author Ernest Hemingway* in order to demonstrate the essential insights these secondary characters provide into the white protagonists while revealing many unspoken particularities of American culture.

The defining features of American literature, she argues, are actually facilitated by a constructed Africanism: "[I]t was this Africanism, deployed as rawness and savagery, that provided the staging ground and arena for the elaboration of the quintessential American identity."[7] If Africanism is at the foundation of American literature, then it is also at the heart of the national identity this literature reflects and helps to maintain. By projecting fears and transgressive desires onto black people through literary Africanism, white Americans also built up a mythology around their own whiteness.

Language and Expression

Key to *Playing in the Dark* is the way Toni Morrison positions herself not only as a critical reader, but as a writer. "As a reader, my assumption had always been that nothing 'happens': Africans and their descendants were not, in any sense that matters, *there*."[8] It is only when she begins to read as a *writer* that she realizes that there is always an Africanist presence lurking behind the text.

If the realization of the hidden importance of the African American in literature depends on Morrison's status as a writer, so does the richly literary style in which the text is written. Think about this passage: "It is as if I had been looking at a fishbowl—the glide and flick of the golden scales ... the tiny, intricate fronds of green ... and suddenly I saw the bowl, the structure that transparently (and invisibly) permits the ordered life it contains to exist in the larger world."[9]

Morrison uses the extended metaphor of the fishbowl to describe the way in which she became aware of the invisible social and literary structures that shape the representation of race in American literature. Beyond this, however, there are many almost novelistic details—the golden scales, the fronds of the water plants—which are not strictly relevant to the point she is making. Perhaps echoing the first word of the book's title, Morrison is "playing" on, and with, her dual status as writer and literary critic. The rich language that emerges from this blurring of the lines between critic and writer may be part of the reason that *Playing in the Dark* appeals to such a wide audience.

NOTES

1   Toni Morrison, *Playing in the Dark: Whiteness and the Literary Imagination* (New York: Vintage Books, 1993), 5.

2   Morrison, *Playing in the Dark*, 12.

3   Morrison, *Playing in the Dark*, 63.

4   Morrison, *Playing in the Dark*, 5.

5   Morrison, *Playing in the Dark*, 6.

6   Willa Cather, *Sapphira and the Slave Girl* (New York: Vintage Books, 2010).

7   Morrison, *Playing in the Dark*, 44.

8   Morrison, *Playing in the Dark*, 17

9   Morrison, *Playing in the Dark*, 17.

MODULE 6
SECONDARY IDEAS

KEY POINTS

- Morrison's readings of racial difference are bound up with her treatment of gender and sexuality; similarly, her interpretation of Africanism* and the American Dream* emerges from her treatment of the Gothic* literary genre.

- While her ideas about genre and national identity are firmly rooted in literary studies, her approach has the potential to engage with many other disciplines.

- The fact that feminism* had become central to literary studies at the time *Playing in the Dark* was written suggested the possibility that race might also become a similarly established element in literary analysis.

Other Ideas

One of the less obvious aspects of Toni Morrison's *Playing in the Dark: Whiteness and the Literary Imagination* is her treatment of gender and sexuality, and how this affects her readings of racial difference. The ways in which feminist ideas have been taken up by writers and academics provides a useful model for the goals Morrison and other scholars of race seek to achieve. For example, feminists linked the use of "he" as a universal pronoun to the maintenance of masculinity as a privileged social position, and their critical interventions have made this practice seem outdated. In *Playing in the Dark,* Morrison suggests that feminism is an essential aspect of reading race in literature, and that its successes set a precedent for race to be incorporated into mainstream literary criticism.

She also discusses how Africanism—certain representations of African American people in the culture of the United States—can be

> 66 The first act of violence that patriarchy demands of males is not violence toward women. Instead patriarchy demands of all males that they engage in acts of psychic self-mutilation, that they kill off the emotional parts of themselves. If an individual is not successful in emotionally crippling himself, he can count on patriarchal men to enact rituals of power that will assault his self-esteem. 99
>
> bell hooks,* *The Will to Change: Men, Masculinity, and Love*

used as a way to explore forbidden or taboo subjects in American society, particularly those surrounding sex and desire. This is closely linked to what Morrison calls "the strong affinity between the nineteenth-century American psyche and the genre of Gothic Romance."[1] Often dealing with desire and the supernatural, Gothic literature is defined by its dark tone; struck by how dark and anxious much early American literature is when compared with the feelings of hope and ambition that drove the colonization of America, Morrison explains this literary love affair with the Gothic in terms of early Americans' fear of the unknown, of failure, and even of freedom itself. Africanist personas became the places onto which white Americans projected these fears.

Exploring the Ideas

In *Playing in the Dark*, Morrison recognizes that gender, like race and class, is a category that is used to distinguish people and divide them into groups that are either free or oppressed. "The presence of black people," she writes, "is inherent, along with gender and family ties, in the earliest lesson every child is taught regarding his or her distinctiveness."[2] Morrison's view of the overlapping oppressions of racism and sexism is born out of the novelist and poet Alice Walker's* suggestion that black women are doubly oppressed, since they have to contend with being perceived as both sexually and racially inferior.

In the final section of the book, however, Morrison extends this idea with a discussion of the way in which "American writers employ an imagined Africanist persona to articulate and imaginatively act out the forbidden in American culture."[3] In other words, writers are able to explore taboos through the figures of African American characters. Many of these forbidden concepts include female sexuality, something that she sees manifested in literature with a mixture of dread and desire.

The third essay in *Playing in the Dark* centers on Morrison's close reading of Ernest Hemingway's* 1937 novel *To Have and Have Not*. Hemingway's protagonist, Harry Morgan, tells his wife that sex with a black woman is "like nurse shark."[4] In doing so, Morrison argues, he is characterizing black women as "the furthest thing from human, so far away as to be not even mammal but fish … Harry's words mark something so brutal, contrary, and alien in its figuration that it does not belong to its own species."[5] The nurturing femininity associated with the word "nurse" is horribly mutated when it is joined to the word "shark": the Africanist persona of the black woman is a vision of monstrous, inhuman femininity.

As the contemporary literature scholar Wendy Steiner* points out: "By making a black woman 'not even mammal,' nor even of 'its own species,' 'nurse shark' commits the same crime that Sethe suffered in [Morrison's 1987 novel] *Beloved*. Pregnant and nursing a child, she was held down in a barn by the white 'Schoolteacher' and his boys, who sucked her milk and contrasted, in neat columns, her human and her animal traits."[6] This is a powerful example of the overlap between Morrison's criticism and her fiction, and the way she harnesses different forms of writing to address similar questions of representation.

The lethal mixture of desire, fear, and objectification that Morrison traces in twentieth-century American Africanist literature has its roots in the transference of anxieties onto slave populations in the literature of the nineteenth century. She writes that "there is no romance free of what [the novelist] Herman Melville called 'the power of blackness,' especially not in a country in which there was a resident population, already black, upon which the imagination could play."[7] White American writers, Morrison suggests, did not need to look for a metaphor for their fears about the unknown, or for their dark desires: black Americans, simultaneously oppressed and feared, were ready-made vessels into which to pour their dread and desire.

Overlooked

While these secondary ideas have sometimes been overlooked by mainstream literary criticism, there have been some moves by critics to apply them to wider issues outside Morrison's remit. The literature scholar Danielle Russell identifies Morrison's stance on the interrelatedness of issues of sex and race with that of the iconic work of feminist criticism *The Madwoman in the Attic* (1979)[8] by the influential feminist literary critics Sandra Gilbert and Susan Gubar.* Russell argues that the issues of sex and race are linked by "the common experience of exclusion and neglect, the consistent failure to address depictions of race and gender in literature and literary criticism."[9] Russell also suggests that Morrison may have overlooked something: "An additional question for Morrison's project might be: does the Africanist presence (directly or indirectly) take a gendered position? That is, is there a masculine Africanist presence that is distinctive from a feminine one?"[10] Although Morrison does engage explicitly with Africanist visions of black women, as we saw above, *Playing in the Dark* does not cover Africanisms specifically bound up with masculinity.

Although Morrison's take on the Gothic and the American Dream has not been followed up by many critics, in 1997 the scholar of American studies and English Teresa Goddu cited it as part of a resurrection of "the term gothic as a critical term in American literary studies."[11] Since then, few scholars have taken up Morrison's ideas about genre and American national identity; this is an avenue of her work in which there is a great deal still to explore.

NOTES

1   Toni Morrison, *Playing in the Dark: Whiteness and the Literary Imagination* (New York: Vintage Books, 1993), 36.

2   Morrison, *Playing in the Dark,* 65

3   Morrison, *Playing in the Dark,* 66

4   Morrison, *Playing in the Dark*, 85.

5   Morrison, *Playing in the Dark.*

6   Wendy Steiner, "The Clearest Eye," *New York Times,* April 5, 1992.

7   Morrison, *Playing in the Dark*, 37.

8   Sandra Gilbert and Susan Gubar, *The Madwoman in the Attic: The Woman Writer and the Nineteenth-Century Literary Imagination* (New Haven, CT: Yale University Press, 1979).

9   Danielle Russell, "Revisiting the Attic," in *Gilbert and Gubar's The Madwoman in the Attic After Thirty Years*, eds. Annette R. Federico and Sandra M. Gilbert (Missouri: University of Missouri Press, 2009), 127–49, 133.

10 Russell, "Revisiting the Attic," 135.

11 Teresa Goddu, *Gothic America: Narrative, History, and Nation* (New York: Columbia University Press, 1997), 8.

MODULE 7
ACHIEVEMENT

KEY POINTS

- Toni Morrison succeeded in writing a best-selling book that changed the way many scholars considered the role of race in the construction of American national identity.

- Morrison's fame as a writer of fiction helped *Playing in the Dark* to reach audiences outside the academic world.

- She has been criticized for failing to mention earlier influential works which also foregrounded race in the formation of American culture.

Assessing The Argument

Toni Morrison's main goal in *Playing in the Dark: Whiteness and the Literary Imagination* was to change the way the majority of literary critics thought about race in literature. She argued that assertions that literature is universal or race-free are not only inaccurate, but actively prevent critics from fully understanding the work of both black and white writers. Not only that, but by ignoring the role that ideas of race have played in creating present-day American national identity, Morrison asserts that racial inequalities continue to be played out both on and off the page.

While her concept of Africanism* has been adopted by some critics, it is still not widely used.[1] Her insistence on the importance of considering whiteness has gained greater traction; the study of race is no longer a matter of considering oppressed ethnic minorities alone. Instead, patterns of racial discrimination have come to be viewed as a formative dialogue between and across races. Whiteness is no longer taken for granted or used as shorthand for the "absence" of race. In its insistence on the importance of reading race between the lines of

> ❝ Morrison's political and pedagogical [i.e. educational] objectives far exceeded the typical demand for the expansion of the canon,* a remedy-through-inclusion of different voices in American arts and letters … Hers was a project in keeping with what some (though certainly not most) progressives in the university saw as nothing less than their intellectual and social responsibility. ❞
>
> Susan Searls Giroux, "Playing in the Dark"

literature and history, *Playing in the Dark* has certainly revolutionized the study of race in literature and in many other disciplines. One key problem with the text, however, is that it fails to acknowledge the vitally important work on race that had been carried out by writers who came before Morrison.

Achievement in Context

Written at a time when a number of scholars were engaged in projects to destabilize established social narratives (that is, to challenge unquestioned assumptions about the nature of society), Morrison's work means that we must now actively rethink notions of race that had traditionally been taken for granted. *Playing in the Dark* brilliantly upends conventional thinking on America's founding principles in light of the omnipresent paradoxes of American life and shows how the constructs of whiteness and blackness are a constant social play with opposites. If values such as freedom, equality, and justice are those that the United States presents to the world on the surface, Morrison flips these to expose the bondage, subjugation, and oppression on the underbelly of this political rhetoric. After reading *Playing in the Dark*, it is almost impossible to view classic American literature without seeing the previously obscured racial subtext* in this body of work.

There can be little doubt that Morrison's status as one of the greatest living American writers—she is both a Pulitzer Prize* winner and a Nobel Laureate*—helped propel what is primarily a work of literary criticism onto the bestseller lists, and onto the bookshelves of non-academics around the world. Since the three essays collected in *Playing in the Dark* started life as lectures, the conversational tone of much of the work and the rich literary language made the book engaging and her ideas easily accessible to non-specialist readers.

Limitations

The accessibility of *Playing in the Dark* has proved key both to the work's success and to the grounds for some of the criticisms that have been leveled against it. Unlike most works of literary criticism, it is under 100 pages long, making it attractive to readers who might find longer works intimidating. The disparity, however, between the book's formidable subject matter—the construction of Africanism and whiteness over the course of hundreds of years of American literature—and the relatively sparse amount of detailed evidence it provides to support its views has provoked questions about its academic rigor from literature scholars such as Danielle Russell.[2]

Playing in the Dark's ideas are influenced by a vast number of thinkers and anti-racist and anti-colonial movements, yet almost none of these are mentioned in the book. Although elsewhere Morrison acknowledges that her ideas about racial representations in the formation of national identity and systems of cultural oppression owe "an obvious debt" to the work of the Palestinian American postcolonialist theorist Edward Said,* neither his name nor any of his publications are explicitly mentioned in the text.[3] Criticisms have also been leveled at the text for overstating its claim about the "whitewashing" of American literature at the hands of mainstream literary scholarship. The English literature scholar Wendy Steiner,* for example, writes that "evidence for Ms. Morrison's Africanism, in fact, turns up everywhere in literary criticism, though piecemeal, seldom expressed with the eloquence and fervor of *Playing in the Dark*. If no systematic study exists of the role black characters play in forming white identity, one could still see a good part of research in black studies and postcolonialism as working toward just this goal."[4]

This assessment makes clear that even if Morrison *has* overstated her case about the absence of studies of whiteness in relation to race in mainstream literary criticism, her work remains an important unifying move in the creation of a strand of critical inquiry dedicated to the analysis of race in literature.

NOTES

1 See Lucille P. Fultz, *Playing with Difference* (Urbana: University of Illinois Press, 2003).

2 See Danielle Russell, "Revisiting the Attic," in *Gilbert and Gubar's The Madwoman in the Attic After Thirty Years*, eds. Annette R. Federico and Sandra M. Gilbert (Missouri: University of Missouri Press, 2009), 127–49.

3 Toni Morrison in Maya Jaggi, "Solving the Riddle," *Guardian*, November 15, 2003.

4 Wendy Steiner, "The Clearest Eye," *New York Times*, April 5, 1992.

MODULE 8
PLACE IN THE AUTHOR'S WORK

KEY POINTS

- Best known for her 11 novels, Toni Morrison is considered one of the greatest living American writers.

- *Playing in the Dark* is Morrison's most widely read work of non-fiction and, like her novels, it is driven by a belief in the power of literature to change society for the better.

- Although much of her reputation rests on the success of her fiction, *Playing in the Dark* is a widely respected work that cements Morrison's position as a scholar as well as a novelist.

Positioning

Toni Morrison's body of work is dominated by her fiction, which includes 11 novels. When she wrote *Playing in the Dark: Whiteness and the Literary Imagination* she had published six of these novels, and had already won the Pulitzer Prize* and the American Book Award* for *Beloved*, published in 1987.[1] All of her novels are concerned with black communities and many of them place these communities at the very center of American cultural identity.[2]

Morrison's novels have consistently displaced the centrality of white narratives, and her characters' journeys often enact the processes by which racialized roles are learned and enforced over individual lifetimes and across generations. *Playing in the Dark* is her first book to approach these issues through the medium of literary criticism. In the book's introduction she makes it clear that her role as a literary critic has been shaped by her position as a writer of fiction. This double position as reader and writer has also influenced the way in which her work has been received by readers both inside and outside the

> ❝ In novels characterized by visionary force and poetic import, [Morrison] gives life to an essential aspect of American reality. ❞
>
> Toni Morrison's Nobel Prize citation in 1993

academic community. Its primary goal may be to change the study of race in literature, but the scope of *Playing in the Dark* extends beyond literary studies, and beyond the academic world, to address the racial inequalities that lie at the heart of present-day America. Morrison's status as a literary giant, leading academic, and public intellectual gives her a platform from which she has been able to highlight the formative effect of race in literature on American national identity.

Integration

Playing in the Dark was written at the pinnacle of Morrison's career, at a moment when her profile as an esteemed academic and public intellectual had begun to match her status as a literary genius. The essays in *Playing in the Dark* were adapted from Morrison's 1992 delivery of the William E. Massey, Sr., Lectures* at Harvard University.* Although this is Morrison's first major work of literary criticism, she has been contributing to this field as an editor and author of shorter pieces for decades. In her position as a senior editor at the prestigious publishing company Random House* in the 1970s, she edited a number of significant publications, including *The Black Book* (1974), which contained reproductions of documents and images from important moments in African American history.[3] By excavating black histories that had been submerged in dominant white accounts of the American past, and by giving voice to previously unheard African Americans in this way, *The Black Book* anticipates the important intervention Morrison makes in *Playing in the Dark*.

In 1990 she published an article titled "Unspeakable Things

Unspoken: The Afro-American Presence in American Literature."[4] This meditated upon many of the same issues of racial representation—such as the impossibility of a "raceless" criticism—that later found full voice in *Playing in the Dark*. In "Unspeakable Things Unspoken" and later in *Playing in the Dark,* she writes that approaching literature as "not only 'universal' but also 'race-free' may have resulted in lobotomizing that literature and in diminishing both the art and the artist."[5]

Significance

Since *Playing in the Dark*, Morrison has edited several collections of essays dealing with race and national identity: *Race-ing Justice, En-gendering Power: Essays on Anita Hill, Clarence Thomas,* and the Construction of Social Reality* (1992); *Birth of a Nation'hood: Gaze, Script, and Spectacle in the O. J. Simpson* Case* (1997); and *Burn This Book: Essay Anthology* (2009).[6] In 2004 she also produced *Remember: The Journey to School Integration,* an anthology of photographs with novelistic captions documenting the process of racial integration in American schools in the 1950s.[7]

Playing in the Dark is both Morrison's most widely read work of non-fiction and also her most influential. So strong are the central themes that run through all of Morrison's work—Africanism,* whiteness, and the effect of history on contemporary African American life—that it is both easy and rewarding to read her fiction and her non-fiction in dialogue with one another. Indeed, perhaps the most common use of *Playing in the Dark*, and one that Morrison may not have predicted, is to help interpret her own fiction. There are several examples of Morrison's methods being used by literary critics to analyze her novels (e.g. Lucille P. Fultz's book *Playing with Difference*).[8]

While its status as a single-authored book of literary criticism marks *Playing in the Dark* apart from the rest of Morrison's prolific body of work, it is entirely consistent with her career-long project of creating bold, poetic, arresting meditations on gender, race, and power that many believe have had a profound and positive influence both on her readers and on the world her work so exquisitely reflects.

NOTES

1   Toni Morrison, *Beloved* (New York: Random House, 2014).

2   Morrison's treatment of race in her fiction is explored in Lucille P. Fultz, *Playing with Difference* (Urbana: University of Illinois Press, 2003).

3   Middleton A. Harris, Morris Levitt, Roger Furman, Ernest Smith, *The Black Book* (New York: Random House, 2009).

4   Toni Morrison, "Unspeakable Things Unspoken: The Afro-American Presence in American Literature," *Michigan Quarterly Review* (Winter 1989), 1–34.

5   Angelyn Mitchell, ed., *Within the Circle: An Anthology of African American Literature* (Durham, NC: Duke University Press, 1994), 379.

6   Toni Morrison, ed., *Race-ing Justice, En-gendering Power: Essays on Anita Hill, Clarence Thomas, and the Construction of Social Reality* (New York: Pantheon Books, 1992); Morrison, ed., *Birth of a Nation'hood: Gaze, Script, and Spectacle in the O. J. Simpson Case* (New York, Pantheon Books: 1997); Morrison, ed., *Burn This Book* (New York: Harper Collins, 2009).

7   Toni Morrison, ed., *Remember: The Journey to School Integration* (New York: Houghton Mifflin, 2004).

8   Fultz, *Playing with Difference*.

SECTION 3
IMPACT

THE FIRST RESPONSES

KEY POINTS

- In addition to being criticized for failing to acknowledge the work of other scholars on race, Toni Morrison's political positioning was called into question, as was her discussion of race as a simplistic black-and-white phenomenon.

- Other critics argued that Morrison's insistence on bringing race into literary studies was timely and important, and that her theorizations of blackness and whiteness were revolutionary.

- The reception of *Playing in the Dark* was always shaped by critics' awareness of Morrison's literary texts.

Criticism

Although the critical response to Toni Morrison's *Playing in the Dark: Whiteness and the Literary Imagination* was overwhelmingly positive, there were critics who identified shortcomings in the work. The literature scholar Anne Stavney* suggested that it was not sufficiently comprehensive, accusing Morrison of ignoring a large body of existing scholarship dealing with race and whiteness, and suggesting that Morrison should acknowledge that other races exist beyond the simplistic black–and–white opposites. The English literature scholar Wendy Steiner,* meanwhile, argued that Morrison's political position in *Playing in the Dark* was unclear.

Stavney argued that Morrison's summary of contemporary literary criticism failed "to provide even a passing nod to the outpouring of literary scholarship in the past decade addressing issues of black and white subjectivity, much less to distinguish between these critical

> ❝ Toni Morrison's commitment to bring race into discussions of American literature ... is united by a ... dissatisfaction with the *representational* framework that still prevails in discussions of black culture [and] black art. ❞
>
> Alessandra Raengo, "Shadowboxing: Lee Daniel's Nonrepresentational Cinema."

projects."[1] Stavney's criticism is that Morrison presents herself as a lone voice and, by omitting references to the many thinkers who went before her and paved the way for her discussions, implicitly positions herself as the first writer to take this position on racial identities. Steiner also questioned Morrison's assertion that race has been overlooked in literary studies, writing that at "a time when conservative scholars and commentators are hammering the humanities for allegedly coercive political correctness, she can hardly fault criticism for reticence about race."[2]

This goes back to the Culture Wars* being fought at American universities at the time when Morrison was writing. Steiner argues that since there was a national argument taking place about "color-blindness"—that is, intentionally ignoring race—Morrison's assertion that critics tended to see literature as raceless was wrong.

Stavney disputed Morrison's use of certain terminology, pointing out contested and vague terms such as "Americanness," "literature," and "American" that appear in the text without any exact explanation of what is meant by them. Most important, for Stavney, is the following question: "Within this definition of American literature, what place is there for literature authored by African-Americans and other non-whites?"[3]

Literature is a famously unstable term (what makes a text literary? Is it down to the way it is written, or how it is read?), and Stavney is arguing that Morrison's argument suffers because she writes about American literature as if it is a known, finite quantity. These questions about the definition of American literature—whether it should be seen to include the work of non-canonical* black and female authors—are central to the Culture Wars.

It is likely that Morrison avoids dealing with such questions about the definition of literature in order to keep *Playing in the Dark* accessible to non-specialist audiences.

Responses

Despite these criticisms, many readers, such as the scholar Shelley Fisher Fishkin,* felt that Morrison's work was a much-needed and learned exploration of race in literature that would have a profound effect on the academic world. Morrison herself has admitted deep intellectual debts to postcolonial* thinkers such as Edward Said,* and many critics have found Stavney's stance on Morrison's lack of engagement with non-African- American non-white authors too hasty.

Donald Klein and Hisham Amin show that Morrison's "methodology can be applied to other works which also rely heavily on racial dynamics, but which are not necessarily broken down along black–white lines."[4] Accordingly, they embark on a long close-reading of representations of whiteness and Native American communities in Ernest Hemingway's* short story "Fathers and Sons," from the collection *Winner Take Nothing* (1933). They conclude that "many of Morrison's concepts can be applied as easily to stories of conquest in the West as they can to stories of slavery in the South, or wherever bodies of literature repeatedly employ 'racially informed and determined chains.'"[5]

Fishkin, meanwhile, countered the claims by critics such as Stavney that Morrison ignored the preexisting emphasis on race in the humanities departments of universities by arguing that she was contributing to developments that were already under way, consciously writing *alongside* what "progressives in the university saw as nothing less than their intellectual and social responsibility."[6] In other words, Morrison's intervention did not ignore the Culture Wars, but was a blow struck as part of them.

Conflict and Consensus

Morrison has said that she listens keenly to what critics have to say about her writing, but that she doesn't always take their advice. In an interview she commented: "I pay them a great deal of attention for several reasons … I want to know whether they know what they're talking about and whether they know what I'm talking about. A very good critical piece is very useful for a writer. A critic should be a conduit, a bridge, but not a law."[7] By this she means that criticism is, for her, a form of communion or communication—a way of engaging in dialogue.

The negative responses from the critics outlined here have been overwhelmingly outnumbered by the hugely positive international responses to this text from writers both inside and outside the academic world. Morrison herself has not responded to critics like Stavney, who expressed anxiety about the limitations of *Playing in the Dark*. The fact that such negative voices are few is also down to the fact that every single critical response to the text operates in dialogue with Morrison's massive body of fiction. Fears about how exhaustive the body of evidence is that Morrison uses in *Playing in the Dark* dissolve when the work is read as part of her lifelong commitment to the discussion of race, history, and American identity. As Fishkin puts it, this is a "brilliant and provocative book" that "no critic of American culture can afford to ignore."[8]

NOTES

1   Anne Stavney, "*Playing in the Dark: Whiteness and Literary Imagination*. By Toni Morrison," in *Studies in the Novel* 26, no. 23 (1994): 328.

2   Wendy Steiner, "The Clearest Eye," *New York Times*, April 5, 1992.

3   Stavney, "*Playing in the Dark*," 329.

4   Donald Klein and Hisham M. Amin, "Racial Legacies," *African American Review* (Winter 1994): 659–63.

5   Klein and Amin, "Racial Legacies"; Toni Morrison, *Playing in the Dark: Whiteness and the Literary Imagination* (New York: Vintage Books, 1993), xi.

6   Susan Searls Giroux, "Playing in the Dark: Racial Repression and the New Campus Crusade for Diversity," *College Literature* 33, no. 4 (2006): 96.

7   Danielle Taylor-Guthrie, ed., *Conversations with Toni Morrison* (Jackson: University Press of Mississippi, 1994), 5.

8   Shelley Fisher Fishkin, "*Playing in the Dark: Whiteness and the Literary Imagination*. By Toni Morrison," *Journal of American History* 80, no. 2 (1993): 629.

MODULE 10
THE EVOLVING DEBATE

KEY POINTS

- Toni Morrison's emphasis on the importance of whiteness helped to cement "whiteness studies"* as a key aspect of research into race in the humanities.

- Her ideas have also promoted advancements in the fields of feminism,* queer theory,* and the study of nationalism.

- *Playing in the Dark* has given rise to new readings of authors such as the nineteenth-century poet and novelist Edgar Allan Poe,* the twentieth-century novelist Edith Wharton,* and the novelist Willa Cather,* and Morrison's critique has been applied to the analysis of race relations in Japanese fiction and representations of Native Americans.

Uses And Problems

Toni Morrison's *Playing in the Dark: Whiteness and the Literary Imagination* has had a distinct influence on the development of literary studies, and in particular on approaches to African American literary criticism.*

According to Morrison, representations of whiteness in American literature are as important as representations of blackness to the study of race in the American imagination, since these concepts are defined *against* and by each other. Furthermore, an unintended consequence of viewing race only in terms of oppressed minorities is that whiteness can be taken for granted; it becomes, in a sense, the normative,* universal, or raceless position. It follows that representations of whiteness in literature can say something about the prevailing social attitudes towards African Americans, even though the text might not mention anything about African American history or culture, or

❝In a body of work spanning five decades Toni
Morrison has engaged in a project for the recovery
and reconstruction of African-American history.
This has involved the creation of a literary aesthetic
through which she exposes hegemonic [i.e. dominant]
and ideological uses of language and knowledge in
the construction and obfuscation [i.e. obscuring]
of American history … It is a political project that
privileges the specificity of African-American
knowledge and linguistic forms and articulates the
history from within which these forms are created. ❞

Justine Baillie, *Toni Morrison and Literary Tradition*

include black characters. Morrison's focus on literary whiteness rather
than on literary blackness helped fuel a new interest in this area. A
section of "Romancing the Shadow," the second essay in *Playing in the
Dark*, formed a central part of the influential whiteness studies
anthology *Critical White Studies: Looking Behind the Mirror*, published in
1997.[1]

Morrison's focus on racial language in the construction of racial
identity (rather than on black or white characters or writers) also
meant that less obvious texts were made available for the application
of African American literary criticism. In this way, Morrison's work
opened up new critical ground, and engendered valuable new
scholarship, including Clare Colquitt, Susan Goodman, and Candace
Waid's *A Forward Glance: New Essays on Edith Wharton* (1999); Ann
Romines's *Willa Cather's Southern Connections: New Essays on Cather in
the South* (2000); and Gerald Kennedy and Liliane Weissberg's
Romancing the Shadow: Poe and Race (2001).[2] All of these texts grew out
of new critical ground cultivated by Morrison's conception of
Africanism* as something that is always present beneath the surface

and in the gaps of American literature.

Schools of Thought

Many scholars of feminism identify with Morrison's attempt to analyze and destabilize dominant cultural narratives. Like her contemporaries and fellow authors Maya Angelou* and Alice Walker,* Morrison approaches the intersections between class, race, and gender in American society, and presents this society from a female Afrocentric* perspective (that is, from a perspective that highlights the concerns of people of African heritage). The Women's Studies scholar Andrea O'Reilly's* *Toni Morrison and Motherhood: A Politics of the Heart* uses Morrison's work as a springboard from which to radically reassess the position of motherhood between racial structures of dominance, arguing alongside Morrison that black motherhood is ultimately a site of personal empowerment and a form of resistance to social oppression. The women's studies and gender studies professor Janet Gray* directly takes up Morrison's project from *Playing in the Dark* in her 2004 book *Race and Time: American Women's Poetics from Anti-Slavery to Racial Modernity.*[3] Using Morrison's theorization of Africanism, Gray examines the ways in which shifting racial identities affect the work of little-studied female American poets of the nineteenth century.

Morrison's practice of reading Africanism into texts that might not seem to consider race on the surface strongly recalls queer theory's practice of *queering*. This is the reading of homosexual or alternative sexual currents into seemingly non-queer literary spaces, and the decentering of normativities—that is, things such as heterosexuality and whiteness that tend to occupy the privileged, "universal" social position. Accordingly, *Playing in the Dark* has given rise to important queer critical interventions such as Robert F. Reid Pharr's* "Tearing the Goat's Flesh; Homosexuality, Abjection, and the Production of a Late Twentieth-Century Black Masculinity" (1995) and Juda Bennett's *Toni Morrison and the Queer Pleasure of Ghosts* (2014).[4]

In *Black Frankenstein: The Making of an American Metaphor* (2008), the English and gender studies scholar Elizabeth Young* draws upon Morrison's theorization of the Gothic* and the American Dream* to argue that the Frankenstein figure in American culture has been a way of voicing anxiety about race and the master–slave relationship. She asserts that this metaphor has continued up until the present day, and is used to represent what is considered to be foreign or threatening by mainstream American culture.[5]

In Current Scholarship

In many ways, Morrison's methodology in *Playing in the Dark* has been as influential as her ideas. The practice of reading race—in particular, ideas of whiteness—into texts that may, superficially, seem focused on other themes has been applied in the analysis of literary representations of other races as well. For example, critics have employed Morrison's critical methods to studies of Native Americans in US literature[6] and to Japanese fiction and history. Sharalyn Orbaugh,* for example, a professor of modern Japanese literature and popular culture, extends Morrison's analysis of submerged racial consciousness in American literature to examine the representation of race between Japanese and Americans in World War II.[7]

Morrison's reputation is still very much rooted in her identity as a novelist; her fiction, scholarship, and social commentary all seem to inform and enrich each other. In the preface to *Playing in the Dark*, Morrison directly identifies the shift that took place when she began "reading as a writer" as a decisive moment in the development of her literary critical position. Advocates of the text, such as the literary theorist Juda Bennett, read her literary criticism and her fiction side by side, arguing that Morrison's role as an author is absolutely essential to an understanding of her critical methods.

NOTES

1   Richard Delgado and Jean Stefancic, eds., *Critical White Studies: Looking Behind the Mirror* (Philadelphia: Temple University Press, 1997).

2   See Gerald Kennedy and Liliane Weissberg, eds., *Romancing the Shadow: Poe and Race* (Oxford: Oxford University Press, 2001); Ann Romines, ed., *Willa Cather's Southern Connections: New Essays on Cather in the South* (Charlottesville: University Press of Virginia, 2000); Clare Colquitt, Susan Goodman, and Candace Waid, eds., *A Forward Glance: New Essays on Edith Wharton* (London: Associated University Presses, 1999).

3   Janet Gray, *Race and Time: American Women's Poetics from Anti-Slavery to Racial Modernity* (Iowa City: Iowa City Press, 2004).

4   Robert F. Reid Pharr, "Tearing the Goat's Flesh; Homosexuality, Abjection, and the Production of a Late Twentieth-Century Black Masculinity," *Studies in the Novel* 28 (1995): 372–94; Juda Bennett, *Toni Morrison and the Queer Pleasure of Ghosts* (New York State University Press, New York: 2014).

5   Elizabeth Young, *Black Frankenstein: The Making of an American Metaphor* (New York: New York University Press, 2008).

6   Donald Klein and Hisham M. Amin, "Racial Legacies," *African American Review* 28, no. 4 (1994): 659–63.

7   Sharalyn Orbaugh, *Japanese Fiction of the Allied Occupation: Vision, Embodiment, Identity* (Lieden: Brill, 2007).

MODULE 11
IMPACT AND INFLUENCE TODAY

KEY POINTS

- Used as a teaching tool, *Playing in the Dark* has given rise to new ways of thinking about race and national identity.

- Issues of racial inequality still haunt the United States, and black voices still struggle to be heard.

- Although race studies have begun to play a more central part in humanities research, the idea of literature and society as "raceless" that Morrison wrote against still prevails in many institutions.

Position

Toni Morrison's *Playing in the Dark: Whiteness and the Literary Imagination* has impacted several areas of academia beyond literary studies, with scholars such as the women's studies professor Danielle Taylor Phillips* profitably applying Morrison's ideas about the construction of race to the discipline of sociology.*[1]

Phillips adopts Morrison's methodology for her archival study of African American domestic workers in the nineteenth and twentieth centuries. By using Morrison's method of reading racial dynamics into seemingly non-racialized texts, Phillips argues that material available in British archives can inform and transform the way scholars approach archive material in New York: reading between the lines of accounts of domestic servitude on both sides of the Atlantic reveals similar patterns of social and racial subjugation.

Playing in the Dark helped propel the process of racial and sexual diversification that was already under way in universities, since Morrison argued that the content of academic courses as well as the

> " [A]dvocates of multiculturalism like Toni Morrison
> ... successfully challenged the contemporary authority
> of Western canons* of thought and aesthetic value,
> interrogated the organization of scholarly disciplines,
> opening up promising routes to new knowledge
> formations, as they more broadly critiqued the notion
> of a 'common culture,' a national identity based on
> homogeneity. "
>
> Susan Searls Giroux, *Between Race and Reason*

teaching process should be designed to include the perspectives of ethnic minorities.[2] Many critics, however, note that this project of reform remains far from complete. As the critical theory scholar Cheryl A. Wall* writes, "given the rise of reactionary politics in the United States at the turn of the twenty-first century, the mission of the university has become even more urgent. But the response to Morrison's clarion call is yet unclear."[3] Wall is referring to the ongoing battles in America about women's rights, gay equality, and America's foreign policy—to say nothing of the relentless socioeconomic and racial inequality that continues to divide the nation.

Interaction

Despite the interventions of generations of activists and thinkers, America remains burdened by racism that is sometimes intentional and overt but more often is manifest in the form of misused racial privilege and microaggressions—acts, either conscious or unconscious, performed by people in positions of social privilege, that serve to cement the existing order in small but significant ways.

Some journalists and cultural critics see the appropriation of aspects of black music and dance by white performers such as the

Australian rapper Iggy Azalea* and the American singer Miley Cyrus,* and the objectification of their black backing dancers (that is, the reduction of their backing singers to objects without agency), as evidence that the mechanics of Africanism* in American artistic culture continue to operate.[4]

There is also a growing resistance to the social and legal materialization of American racism, from economic redlining (the strategic denial of financial products such as mortgages or loans to minority communities) to police shootings of unarmed African Americans. Within these movements, disagreement remains over the means of achieving the necessary social change now that racial oppression is largely a matter of custom rather than law (since the abolition of slavery and the dismantling of the segregation laws).

Justice Clarence Thomas*—the second-ever, and currently the only, black justice of the highest legal body in the United States, the Supreme Court—is in favor of a color-blind approach as he believes that differentiation between races produces "a cult of victimization" and causes black people to believe that they need "special treatment in order to succeed."[5] This is the attitude that Morrison and others were writing against during the Culture Wars*—the sense that racial inequality can be best dealt with by pretending that it does not exist. Because there is no objective, biological basis for "race," ignoring the social reality of people marked as racially inferior is an easy option and one that, the opponents of "color-blindness" argue, allows racial oppression to continue.

The lifelong conversation about race in which Morrison has been trying to engage America continues. For Morrison, the university holds great potential as a setting for the advancement of new ideas and strategies to help us understand, confront, and ultimately overcome racial inequality. She recently argued that "if the university does not take seriously and rigorously its role as guardian of wider civic freedoms … then some other regime or ménage of regimes will do it for us, in spite of us, and without us."[6]

The Continuing Debate

In recent years there has been a spate of killings of black people in the United States, often at the hands of the police, very few of whom face any form of punishment. One of the first such cases to receive global attention happened in 2013, when neighborhood watch coordinator George Zimmerman was acquitted for the lethal shooting in Sanford, Florida of the African American teenager Trayvon Martin. In 2014, 18-year-old Michael Brown was shot dead while unarmed (and, witnesses allege, with his hands in the air) in Ferguson, Missouri by police officer Darren Wilson, prompting civil unrest in Ferguson and protests around the world. These and other prominent cases prompted the rise of grassroots movements such as the Black Lives Matter campaign. If it was important to address the dehumanizing effects of racial power dynamics in 1992 when Morrison wrote *Playing in the Dark*, it is even more politically urgent to do so now.

Proponents of a race-conscious, rather than color-blind, approach to thinking about race in society recognize a vital link between representations of race and real lived experience. As Morrison explains in a recent interview, one of the protagonists of her latest novel, *God Help the Child* (2015), becomes a postgraduate economics student because "he finds the African-American Studies department fails to address a simple proposition: that 'most of the real answers concerning slavery, lynching, forced labor, sharecropping, racism, Jim Crow,* prison labor, migration, civil rights and black revolution movements were all about money.'"[7]

This idea of the failure of the American academic world to engage with issues of race is as strong in Morrison's writing today as it was in *Playing in the Dark* and in her early novels. The link between what is studied and what is *lived* remains one of Morrison's primary concerns.

NOTES

1   Danielle Taylor Phillips, "Moving with the Women: Tracing Racialization, Migration, and Domestic Workers in the Archive," *Signs Journal of Women in Culture and Society*, 38, no. 2 (2013): 379–404.

2   See Susan Searls Giroux, "Playing in the Dark: Racial Repression and the New Campus Crusade for Diversity," *College Literature* 33, no. 4 (2006): 96.

3   Cheryl A. Wall, "Toni Morrison, Editor and Teacher," in *The Cambridge Companion to Toni Morrison*, ed. Justine Tally (Cambridge: Cambridge University Press, 2007), 147.

4   See Hadley Freeman, "Miley Cyrus's Twerking Routine was Cultural Appropriation at its Worst," *Guardian*, August 27, 2013; Jennifer Pozner, John McWhorter, Adrienne Keene, Jamia Wilson, and Laia Garcia, "Whose Culture Is It, Anyhow?" *New York Times*, August 4, 2015.

5   "Clarence Thomas: The Justice Nobody Knows," CBS interview, September 27, 2007.

6   Toni Morrison, "How Can Values be Taught in the University?" *Michigan Quarterly Review* 40, no. 2 (2001): 278.

7   Gaby Wood, "Toni Morrison Interview: On Racism, Her New Novel and Marlon Brando," *Daily Telegraph*, April 19, 2015.

MODULE 12
WHERE NEXT?

KEY POINTS

- The increase in state-sanctioned violence against African Americans suggests that finding lasting solutions to racial inequality is even more urgent now than it was when Morrison wrote *Playing in the Dark*.

- The continued use of Morrison's literary theory in universities has the potential to change the way new generations of readers, writers, and scholars consider race and identity.

- *Playing in the Dark* has revolutionized the way race is considered in academia, and has brought critical ideas about whiteness and national identity to audiences outside university classrooms.

Potential

Toni Morrison is a passionate believer in the power of education to effect social change, viewing the university in particular as the "guardian of … civic freedoms."[1] With this in mind, the inclusion of *Playing in the Dark: Whiteness and the Literary Imagination* in university syllabuses in literary studies, creative writing, history, sociology,* and women's studies must be reassuring to her.

If *Playing in the Dark* continues to be studied, and if universities possess the transformative power with which Morrison credits them, the text looks set to shape the way young people think about race in the future. As protest movements against police violence and racial discrimination continue to grow, as the gap in socioeconomic conditions between black and white communities widens, and as manifestations of racism continue to appear in civil society and popular

> ❝ For [Morrison] ... the critical analysis of literature and culture is more than an academic exercise; it is part of the battle over representations of race, gender, and class in the United States that has the potential to shape social and political practices. ❞
>
> Linda Krumholz, "Playing in the Dark"

culture, *Playing in the Dark* is more valuable than ever. The way Morrison's critique enables black experience to be read back into a history and culture that sought to characterize it as irrelevant stands to add force to present-day resistance movements. The book's status as a "crossover" text, accessible to academic communities and non-specialist audiences alike, means that its appeal easily extends to anyone who seeks to challenge inequality in twenty-first-century America.

Morrison's work has proved hugely versatile—both in terms of her critical method, and in its foregrounding of the development of racial identity as a dialogue between races. Beyond the influence *Playing in the Dark* has had on literary studies, history, race studies, and intersectional* feminism* (intersectionality being an approach to the analysis of oppression that considers the places where different forms of oppression overlap), its methodological contribution to the fields of sociology and queer theory* looks likely to continue to bear fruit. Wherever there are patterns of oppression—whether because of race, religion, sexuality, or other forms of difference—*Playing in the Dark* will remain an indispensable resource for thinkers wishing to understand and reform the social structures they live within and help create.

Future Directions

In a world rife with religious and racial conflict, and growing economic inequality, Toni Morrison's *Playing in the Dark* is increasingly relevant to the lived experience of people around the world.

Postcolonial* critics such as Anna Bernard,* whose recent book *Rhetorics of Belonging: Nation, Narration, and Israel/Palestine* deals with the role of literature in the formation of Israeli–Palestinian national identities, are making valuable new contributions to their field by taking up Morrison's critical baton.[2]

Similarly, scholars such as Claire Chambers,* who examines the role of Muslims in the construction of British identities, and critiques Islamophobia* (that is, anti-Muslim sentiment), are part of the next generation of thinkers to gain new understandings of the world by examining the representations of identities held to be "normal" and the representation of identities held to be "different to the normal" in the context of a system of oppression.[3]

The scope for interventions along these lines extends across the boundaries of academic disciplines and beyond the borders of the university. Aside from grassroots political movements protesting inequality, it seems likely that many more novelists and practitioners of other art forms will continue to be inspired by Morrison's commitment to reinterpreting the formation of ideas of difference in the past to avoid reproducing oppressive power dynamics in the present.

Summary

Playing in the Dark stresses the role that African Americans, and the web of negative associations projected upon them, had in the creation of American national identity. Morrison insists that the study of race should focus not just on the way minority races are represented, but on how white American identity is tightly bound to limiting constructs of the African American persona. Over the span of three short essays, she radically rethinks the history of America and its literature, arguing that even where African Americans seem to be incidental to a work of literature, Africanism*—representations of black American people—is a deep shaping factor in the creation of the American psyche and therefore is always present. More, within Morrison's framework, race doesn't disappear when black characters are absent; she upsets the commonplace equation of whiteness with racelessness or universality.

Whether Africanism appears as a metaphor for the fear of the unknown by nineteenth-century Gothic* novelists, or as a means of exploring mingled fantasies and nightmares of female sexuality and maternity in twentieth-century texts, Morrison shows that white America has, in the "dark" of its unconscious imagination, defined itself in opposition to the Africanist "other." Her condemnation of the way American literary criticism effectively whitewashes American literature—using political correctness and polite convention to avoid acknowledging the presence of race—is intensely political, and formed an important part of the Culture Wars* of the 1990s. Morrison's work has had an impact on many schools of thought beyond literary studies, and has helped to make race a central part of present-day studies in the humanities.

Throughout *Playing in the Dark* and in her fiction, Morrison stresses the importance of resurrecting the submerged history and significance of African Americans, and of expanding the way we think about the problems of race; the question is not simply a matter of those who are oppressed by racism.

In doing so, she suggests, we have the ability to garner a more sophisticated understanding of the inequalities of the present, and to begin to redress the imbalances between people of different races that continue to violently disrupt and divide our world.

NOTES

1   Toni Morrison, "How Can Values be Taught in the University?" *Michigan Quarterly Review* 40, no. 2 (2001): 278.

2   Anna Bernard, *Rhetorics of Belonging: Nation, Narration, and Israel/ Palestine* (Liverpool University Press, Liverpool: 2013).

3   Claire Chambers, *Britain through Muslim Eyes: Literary Representations, 1780–1988*. (Basingstoke: Palgrave Macmillan, 2015).

GLOSSARY

GLOSSARY OF TERMS

African American literary criticism: a school of literary studies that reads (typically American) literature in the light of African American history, culture, and experience.

Africanism: this is Morrison's term for a pattern of representing African Americans. Her idea of Africanism is more than a description of skin color or ethnic background; instead, it encompasses the many layers of negative associations, fears, and anxieties projected onto black people, which allows white America to define itself as its opposite.

Afrocentric: being focused on African concerns, or the concerns of those with African heritage.

American Academy of Arts and Letters: an institution established in 1904. Members of the academy are chosen for life and are some of the leading figures in literature, theatre, art, and film. These members award annual monetary prizes to emerging artists.

American Book Awards: an annual American writers' award given by other writers in recognition of "outstanding literary achievement," regardless of race, sex, ethnic background, or gender.

American Dream: a collection of ideals at the heart of American national identity that encompasses the idea that anyone, no matter how underprivileged their start in life, can achieve upward social mobility and personal happiness.

Black Arts Movement: a movement of the 1960s and 1970s partly established by black nationalism and the Civil Rights Movement. It was based on a set of theories called the "black aesthetic" that encouraged African Americans to create a popular culture that was distinct from white culture. Many of its advocates established racially separate publishing houses, theatre troupes, and study groups.

Black Power Movement: an African American movement of the 1960s and 1970s marked by a political radicalism that sometimes brought it into opposition with the Civil Rights Movement. It is often understood to be founded on principles such as black nationalism and separatism.

Canonical: works deemed to be the most important of a particular time or place.

Civil Rights Movement: the name given to the mid-twentieth-century social movements that aimed to end racial segregation, voting restrictions, and workplace discrimination, and to secure equal rights for all Americans.

Cornell University: a highly selective university in Ithaca, New York.

Culture Wars: a conflict among American intellectuals in the 1990s. Some believed that American culture needed to be opened up to consider the cultural contributions of minorities, while others contended that the core, Eurocentric values of American culture had to be maintained.

Feminism: a term that encompasses a range of movements centered on achieving equality between men and women, and the campaign for equal political, social, and economic rights for women.

Gothic romance: a genre of literature that was especially popular in the eighteenth and nineteenth centuries. Gothic romance novelists were interested in the supernatural and in evoking feelings of fear, awe, and often desire in the reader.

Harlem Renaissance: a cultural movement between 1919 and 1937 that sought to encourage pride within the African American community, and to explore what made this community culturally unique. It incorporated art, theatre, music, and literature, and in many ways helped to usher in the Civil Rights Movement.

Harvard University: established in 1636 and located in Cambridge, Massachusetts, this private institution is regarded as one of the most prestigious universities in the world.

Homophobia: negative attitudes and feelings toward lesbian, gay, bisexual, and transgender people.

Howard University: a distinguished institution, open to both sexes and all races, which has historically been a university for black students; it was established in 1867 and is located in Washington, DC.

Intersectionality: the study of overlapping forms of oppression and subjugation. In this framework, women of color (for example) exist at the intersection of oppression based on race *and* gender.

Islamophobia: the hatred of—or prejudice against—Muslims.

Jim Crow Laws: a system of rules put in place after the abolition of slavery that segregated public spaces and institutions such as schools and hospitals along racial lines.

Nobel Prize in literature: an annual prize awarded to an author from any country who has produced an outstanding body of literary work. This is considered the highest award for lifetime achievement in the world of literature.

Normative: a term relating to an ideal standard or model, or what is thought of as the normal way of doing something.

Postcolonialism: a school of criticism founded in the 1970s concerned with the history, culture, politics, and economics of countries and people suffering from colonial occupation and its legacies.

Presidential Medal of Freedom: an award given by the president of the United States to an individual who has made a significant contribution to the country's security, peace, or culture. The highest civilian award available in the United States, it can also be given to military personnel and those who are not American citizens.

Princeton University: established in 1747 and located in the town of Princeton, New Jersey, this is one of the leading educational institutions in the world.

Pulitzer Prize for fiction: one of seven Pulitzer Prizes. The prize for fiction is given annually to American writers, typically those who deal with some aspect of American life.

Queer theory: a school of criticism that emerged in the 1990s based on gay/lesbian studies and women's studies. While gay/lesbian studies are concerned with representations of homosexuality in culture, queer theory looks at any kind of sexual practice or identity that crosses what conservative society deems "normal."

Random House: a publishing company based in New York City. It is the largest general interest trade book publisher in the world.

Reagan–Bush era: Ronald Reagan served as president of the United States from 1981 to 1989, and his vice-president George Bush succeeded him as president from 1989 to 1993. The Reagan–Bush era is the time during which these two Republican politicians were in power.

Romance: used by Morrison as a term to refer to literary works of the Romantic period in the late eighteenth and early nineteenth century. Romanticism was an artistic movement interested in exploring human emotions and the way they engage with the landscape; it is often seen to be a reaction against industrialization.

Second-wave feminism: a feminist movement that extended approximately from the 1960s to the 1980s. As with the first wave of this movement, which centered on women's suffrage, it was primarily concerned with obtaining equal rights for women. A distinctive element of the second-wave movement was that cultural and political inequalities were seen as inextricably linked.

Sociology: the study of the history, structure, and functioning of human society.

Subtext: meaning in a text that must be inferred by the reader.

Whiteness studies: a controversial branch of Critical Race Studies developed in the United States in the late twentieth century. It investigates whiteness as a social construct and challenges racial privilege by refusing to position whiteness as racially neutral.

William E. Massey, Sr., Lectures in the History of American Civilization: a series of public talks held at Harvard University since 1984 and delivered by highly respected scholars.

PEOPLE MENTIONED IN THE TEXT

Maya Angelou (1928–2014) was an African American author and poet. She is best known for her series of seven autobiographies, including *I Know Why the Caged Bird Sings* (1969).

Iggy Azalea (b. 1990) is an Australian rapper and songwriter.

Anna Bernard is lecturer in English literature at the Department of English and Comparative Literature at King's College London. Her book *Rhetorics of Belonging: Nation, Narration, and Israel/Palestine* (2013) explores the way Israeli and Palestinian writers engage with the expectation that they should tell the story of their nations.

Harold Bloom (b. 1930) is an American literary critic and professor at Yale. His book *The Western Canon* (1994) argues that literary criticism should not be political and has often been cited by critics who counter the argument that minority writers should be included in the literary canon.

George Bush (b. 1924) was the 41st president of the United States. He was a Republican, and like that of Reagan before him, his government privileged integration over multiculturalism.

W. E. B. Du Bois (1868–1963) was a sociologist, historian, author, and civil rights activist. His book *The Souls of Black Folk* (1903) was one of the first sociological explorations of the African American experience.

Willa Cather (1873–1947) was a female American novelist. She won the 1927 Pulitzer Prize for fiction for her novel *One of Ours*.

Claire Chambers is lecturer in global literature in the English and Related Literature Department of the University of York. She is best known for her book *British Muslim Fictions: Interviews with Contemporary Writers* (2011), and for her work examining the construction of Muslim identities in Britain.

Miley Cyrus (b. 1992) is an American singer and actor. Her father is the singer Billy Ray Cyrus.

Shelley Fisher Fishkin is a scholar of Humanities and American Studies with a focus on marginalized voices in US literature.

Michel Foucault (1926–1984) was an influential French philosopher, historian of ideas, and literary critic. His work examined the relationship between knowledge and power, and the roles they play in controlling societies.

Henry Louis Gates, Jr. (b. 1950) is an African American literary critic and academic, currently based at Harvard University. He has written 17 books and created 14 documentary films about black history and race relations in the United States.

Sandra Gilbert (b. 1936) and Susan Gubar (b.1944) are American literary critics and academics. They are best known for their seminal work of feminist criticism *The Madwoman in the Attic: The Woman Writer and the Nineteenth-Century Literary Imagination* (1979), which looks at Victorian literature from a feminist perspective.

Janet Gray is a professor of women's and gender studies who writes on gender and race in the United States in the years before and after the American Civil War of 1861–65.

Ernest Hemingway (1899–1961) was an American author and journalist. He is widely considered to be one of the greatest American writers, and won the Nobel Prize in literature in 1954.

bell hooks (b. 1952) is the pen name of Gloria Jean Watkins, a prominent public intellectual, social justice activist and author of over 30 books. Her work focuses on the connection between race, gender, and class through the analysis of popular films, music, and literature.

Harold Morrison is a Jamaican architect who married Toni Morrison in 1958. Although they divorced in 1964, Toni kept her married name.

Sharalyn Orbaugh is a professor of modern Japanese literature and popular culture with a focus on postwar Japanese women's fiction.

Andrea O'Reilly (b. 1961) is a scholar of Women's Studies with a focus on women, the body, and motherhood.

Robert F. Reid Pharr (b. 1965) is an essayist and professor in critical race studies and queer theory.

Danielle Taylor Phillips is a professor of women's studies whose research and writing centers on the intersection of gender, race, and class.

Edgar Allan Poe (1809–1849) was an American poet and short-story writer. His work is steeped in the Gothic, and he is sometimes credited with inventing the genre of detective fiction.

Ronald Reagan (1911–2004) was the 40th president of the United States. His government was in favor of color-blindness—the idea that race should not be a factor in governance.

Edward Said (1935–2003) was a Palestinian American cultural theorist and one of the founders of postcolonial studies. *Orientalism* (1978), his most influential work, examines the role that Western literary representations of the East have played in constructing the patterns of racial, cultural, and religious inequality that continue to divide the world.

Arthur M. Schlesinger, Jr., (1917–2007) was an American historian, social critic, and public intellectual. After working as an academic and as Special Assistant to President John F. Kennedy, he became Professor of Humanities at The City University of New York. He is best known for his book *The Disuniting of America* (1991), which contested multiculturalism.

Barbara Smith (b. 1946) is an African American academic, socialist, and feminist. She has played a significant role in establishing black feminism in the United States.

Anne Stavney is a literary critic and scholar whose research focuses on representations of women of color in twentieth-century fiction.

Wendy Steiner (b. 1949) is a professor of contemporary literature and critical theory.

Clarence Thomas (b. 1948) is an African American associate justice of the Supreme Court of the United States. The second African American ever to serve on it, he is considered one of the most conservative voices in the Supreme Court.

Cheryl A. Wall (b. 1948) is a professor of English and critical theory specializing in the Harlem Renaissance.

Alice Walker (b. 1944) is an American novelist, literary critic, poet, and activist. She is best known for her 1984 novel *The Color Purple*, for which she won the Pulitzer Prize for fiction and the National Book Award.

Edith Wharton (1862–1937) was an American writer and designer. She was nominated for the Nobel Prize in literature in 1927, 1928, and 1930.

Elizabeth Young is a scholar of English and gender studies. Her scholarship analyzes intersections of gender, race, and sexuality in American culture.

WORKS CITED

WORKS CITED

Baillie, Justine. *Toni Morrison and Literary Tradition: the Invention of an Aesthetic*. London & New York: Bloomsbury Academic, 2013.

Bennett, Juda. *Toni Morrison and the Queer Pleasure of Ghosts*. New York: New York State University Press, 2014.

Bernard, Anna. *Rhetorics of Belonging: Nation, Narration, and Israel/Palestine*. Liverpool: Liverpool University Press, 2013.

Bloom, Harold. *The Western Canon: The Books and School of the Ages*. London: Macmillan, 1995.

Cather, Willa. *Sapphira and the Slave Girl*. New York: Vintage Books, 2010.

Chambers, Claire. *Britain through Muslim Eyes: Literary Representations, 1780–1988*. Basingstoke: Palgrave Macmillan, 2015.

"Clarence Thomas: The Justice Nobody Knows". CBS interview, 27 September 2007.

Colquitt, Clare, Susan Goodman, and Candace Waid, eds. *A Forward Glance: New Essays on Edith Wharton*. London: Associated University Presses, 1999.

Du Bois, W. E. B. *The Souls of Black Folk*. Chicago: A. C. McClurg, 1903.

Fishkin, Shelley Fisher. "*Playing in the Dark: Whiteness and the Literary Imagination*. By Toni Morrison." *Journal of American History* 80, no. 2 (1993): 629.

Freeman, Hadley. "Miley Cyrus's Twerking Routine was Cultural Appropriation at its Worst." *Guardian*, August 27, 2013.

Fultz, Lucille P. *Playing with Difference*. Urbana: University of Illinois Press, 2003.

Gates, Jr., Henry Louis. *Figures in Black: Words, Signs, and the "Racial" Self*. New York: Oxford University Press, 1987.

Gilbert, Sandra and Susan Gubar. *The Madwoman in the Attic: The Woman Writer and the Nineteenth-Century Literary Imagination*. New Haven, CT: Yale University Press, 1979.

Giroux, Susan Searls. *Between Race and Reason: Violence, Intellectual Responsibility and the University to Come*. Stanford, CA: Stanford University Press, 2010.

———. "Playing in the Dark: Racial Repression and the New Campus Crusade for Diversity." *College Literature* 33, no. 4 (2006): 93–112.

Goddu, Teresa. *Gothic America: Narrative, History, and Nation.* New York: Columbia University Press: 1997.

Gray, Janet. *Race and Time: American Women's Poetics from Anti-Slavery to Racial Modernity.* Iowa City: Iowa University Press, 2004.

Griffith, Glyne. "Reading in the Dark: Race, Literature, and the Discourse of Blackness." In *Color, Hair, and Bone: Race in the Twenty-first Century*, edited by Linden Lewis, Glyne A. Griffith, and Elizabeth Crespo Kebler, 29–46. Cranbury, NJ: Associate University Presses, 2008.

Harris, Middleton A., Morris Levitt, Roger Furman, and Ernest Smith. *The Black Book.* New York: Random House, 2009.

Hooks, Bell. The Will To Change: Men, Masculinity, and Love. New York: Atria Books, 2004.

Jaggi, Maya. "Solving the Riddle." *Guardian*, 15 November 2003.

Kennedy, Gerald, and Liliane Weissberg, eds. *Romancing the Shadow: Poe and Race.* Oxford: Oxford University Press, 2001.

Klein, Donald, and Hisham M. Amin. "Racial Legacies." *African American Review* 28, no. 4 (1994): 659–63.

Krumholz, Linda. "Toni Morrison's *Playing in the Dark: Whiteness and the Literary Imagination*." *Signs* 1 (1996): 243–8.

Lester, R. K. "An Interview with Toni Morrison, Hessian Radio Network, Frankfurt, West Germany." In *Critical Essays on Toni Morrison*, edited by Nellie Y. McKay, 47–54. Boston: G. K. Hall, 1988.

Maher, Frances A., and Mary Kay Thompson Tetreault. *The Feminist Classroom: Dynamics of Gender, Race, and Privilege*. Lanham, MD: Rowman & Littlefield, 2001.

Matus, Jill. *Toni Morrison*. Manchester: Manchester University Press, 1998.

McKay, Nellie, ed.. *Critical Essays on Toni Morrison*. Boston: G. K. Hall, 1988.

Mitchell, Angelyn, ed. *Within the Circle: An Anthology of African American Literature*. Durham, NC: Duke University Press, 1994.

Morrison, Toni. *Beloved*. New York: Random House, 2014.

———. *God Help the Child*. New York: Random House, 2015.

———. "Loose Magic: A. J. Verdelle Interviews Toni Morrison." In *Toni Morrison: Conversations*, edited by Carolyn C. Denard, 159–70. Jackson: University of Mississippi Press, 2008.

———. *Playing in the Dark: Whiteness and the Literary Imagination*. New York: Vintage Books, 1993.

————. "Unspeakable Things Unspoken: The Afro-American Presence in American Literature." *Michigan Quarterly Review* (1989): 1–34.

————, ed. *Birth of a Nation'hood: Gaze, Script, and Spectacle in the O. J. Simpson Case*. New York, Pantheon Books: 1997.

————, ed. *Burn This Book*. New York: Harper Collins, 2009.

————, ed. *Race-ing Justice, En-gendering Power: Essays on Anita Hill, Clarence Thomas, and the Construction of Social Reality*. New York: Pantheon Books, 1992.

————, ed. *Remember: The Journey to School Integration*. New York: Houghton Mifflin, 2004.

Moses, Cathy. *Dissenting Fictions: Identity and Resistance in the Contemporary American Novel*. New York: Routledge, 2013.

Orbaugh, Sharalyn. *Japanese Fiction of the Allied Occupation: Vision, Embodiment, Identity*. Lieden: Brill, 2007.

O'Reilly, Andrea. *Toni Morrison and Motherhood: A Politics of the Heart*. New York: State University of New York Press, 2004.

Pharr, Robert F. Reid. "Tearing the Goat's Flesh: Homosexuality, Abjection and The Production of a Late Twentieth-Century Black Masculinity." *Studies in the Novel* 28 (1995): 372–94.

Phillips, Danielle Taylor. "Moving with the Women: Tracing Racialization, Migration, and Domestic Workers in the Archive." *Signs* 38, no. 2 (2013): 379–404.

Pozner, Jennifer, John McWhorter, Adrienne Keene, Jamia Wilson, and Laia Garcia. "Whose Culture Is It, Anyhow?" *New York Times*, August 4, 2015.

Raengo, Alessandra. "Shadowboxing: Lee Daniel's Nonrepresentational Cinema." In *Contemporary Black American Cinema: Race, Gender and Sexuality at the Movies*, edited by Mia Mask, 200–216. Abingdon: Routledge, 2012.

Romines, Ann, ed. *Willa Cather's Southern Connections: New Essays on Cather in the South*. Charlottesville: University Press of Virginia, 2000.

Royan, Tessa, ed. *Cambridge Introduction to Toni Morrison*. Cambridge: Cambridge University Press, 2013.

Russell, Danielle. "Revisiting the Attic". In *Gilbert and Gubar's The Madwoman in the Attic After Thirty Years*, edited by Annette R. Federico and Sandra M. Gilbert, 127–49. Missouri: University of Missouri Press, 2009.

Said, Edward. *Orientalism*. New York: Random House, 1979.

Schlesinger Jr., Michael M. *The Disuniting of America: Reflections on a Multicultural Society*. New York: Norton & Company, 1998.

Steiner, Wendy. "The Clearest Eye." *New York Times*, April 5, 1992.

Taylor-Guthrie, Danielle, ed. *Conversations with Toni Morrison*. Jackson: University Press of Mississippi, 1994.

Uetricht, Micah. "The Culture Wars Are Over—And They Are Not Coming Back". *In These Times*, June 11, 2015. Accessed September 30, 2015. http://inthesetimes.com/article/18022/culture_wars_andrew_hartman.

Wall, Cheryl A. "Toni Morrison, Editor and Teacher." In *The Cambridge Companion to Toni Morrison*, edited by Justine Tally. Cambridge: Cambridge University Press, 2007.

Wood, Gaby. "Toni Morrison Interview: On Racism, Her New Novel and Marlon Brando." *Daily Telegraph*, 19 April 2015.

Young, Elizabeth. *Black Frankenstein: The Making of an American Metaphor*. New York: New York University Press, 2008.

THE MACAT LIBRARY
BY DISCIPLINE

AFRICANA STUDIES

Chinua Achebe's *An Image of Africa: Racism in Conrad's Heart of Darkness*
W. E. B. Du Bois's *The Souls of Black Folk*
Zora Neale Huston's *Characteristics of Negro Expression*
Martin Luther King Jr's *Why We Can't Wait*
Toni Morrison's *Playing in the Dark: Whiteness in the American Literary Imagination*

ANTHROPOLOGY

Arjun Appadurai's *Modernity at Large: Cultural Dimensions of Globalisation*
Philippe Ariès's *Centuries of Childhood*
Franz Boas's *Race, Language and Culture*
Kim Chan & Renée Mauborgne's *Blue Ocean Strategy*
Jared Diamond's *Guns, Germs & Steel: the Fate of Human Societies*
Jared Diamond's *Collapse: How Societies Choose to Fail or Survive*
E. E. Evans-Pritchard's *Witchcraft, Oracles and Magic Among the Azande*
James Ferguson's *The Anti-Politics Machine*
Clifford Geertz's *The Interpretation of Cultures*
David Graeber's *Debt: the First 5000 Years*
Karen Ho's *Liquidated: An Ethnography of Wall Street*
Geert Hofstede's *Culture's Consequences: Comparing Values, Behaviors, Institutes and Organizations across Nations*
Claude Lévi-Strauss's *Structural Anthropology*
Jay Macleod's *Ain't No Makin' It: Aspirations and Attainment in a Low-Income Neighborhood*
Saba Mahmood's *The Politics of Piety: The Islamic Revival and the Feminist Subject*
Marcel Mauss's *The Gift*

BUSINESS

Jean Lave & Etienne Wenger's *Situated Learning*
Theodore Levitt's *Marketing Myopia*
Burton G. Malkiel's *A Random Walk Down Wall Street*
Douglas McGregor's *The Human Side of Enterprise*
Michael Porter's *Competitive Strategy: Creating and Sustaining Superior Performance*
John Kotter's *Leading Change*
C. K. Prahalad & Gary Hamel's *The Core Competence of the Corporation*

CRIMINOLOGY

Michelle Alexander's *The New Jim Crow: Mass Incarceration in the Age of Colorblindness*
Michael R. Gottfredson & Travis Hirschi's *A General Theory of Crime*
Richard Herrnstein & Charles A. Murray's *The Bell Curve: Intelligence and Class Structure in American Life*
Elizabeth Loftus's *Eyewitness Testimony*
Jay Macleod's *Ain't No Makin' It: Aspirations and Attainment in a Low-Income Neighborhood*
Philip Zimbardo's *The Lucifer Effect*

ECONOMICS

Janet Abu-Lughod's *Before European Hegemony*
Ha-Joon Chang's *Kicking Away the Ladder*
David Brion Davis's *The Problem of Slavery in the Age of Revolution*
Milton Friedman's *The Role of Monetary Policy*
Milton Friedman's *Capitalism and Freedom*
David Graeber's *Debt: the First 5000 Years*
Friedrich Hayek's *The Road to Serfdom*
Karen Ho's *Liquidated: An Ethnography of Wall Street*

The Macat Library By Discipline

John Maynard Keynes's *The General Theory of Employment, Interest and Money*
Charles P. Kindleberger's *Manias, Panics and Crashes*
Robert Lucas's *Why Doesn't Capital Flow from Rich to Poor Countries?*
Burton G. Malkiel's *A Random Walk Down Wall Street*
Thomas Robert Malthus's *An Essay on the Principle of Population*
Karl Marx's *Capital*
Thomas Piketty's *Capital in the Twenty-First Century*
Amartya Sen's *Development as Freedom*
Adam Smith's *The Wealth of Nations*
Nassim Nicholas Taleb's *The Black Swan: The Impact of the Highly Improbable*
Amos Tversky's & Daniel Kahneman's *Judgment under Uncertainty: Heuristics and Biases*
Mahbub Ul Haq's *Reflections on Human Development*
Max Weber's *The Protestant Ethic and the Spirit of Capitalism*

FEMINISM AND GENDER STUDIES

Judith Butler's *Gender Trouble*
Simone De Beauvoir's *The Second Sex*
Michel Foucault's *History of Sexuality*
Betty Friedan's *The Feminine Mystique*
Saba Mahmood's *The Politics of Piety: The Islamic Revival and the Feminist Subjec*t
Joan Wallach Scott's *Gender and the Politics of History*
Mary Wollstonecraft's *A Vindication of the Rights of Woman*
Virginia Woolf's *A Room of One's Own*

GEOGRAPHY

The Brundtland Report's *Our Common Future*
Rachel Carson's *Silent Spring*
Charles Darwin's *On the Origin of Species*
James Ferguson's *The Anti-Politics Machine*
Jane Jacobs's *The Death and Life of Great American Cities*
James Lovelock's *Gaia: A New Look at Life on Earth*
Amartya Sen's *Development as Freedom*
Mathis Wackernagel & William Rees's *Our Ecological Footprint*

HISTORY

Janet Abu-Lughod's *Before European Hegemony*
Benedict Anderson's *Imagined Communities*
Bernard Bailyn's *The Ideological Origins of the American Revolution*
Hanna Batatu's *The Old Social Classes And The Revolutionary Movements Of Iraq*
Christopher Browning's *Ordinary Men: Reserve Police Batallion 101 and the Final Solution in Poland*
Edmund Burke's *Reflections on the Revolution in France*
William Cronon's *Nature's Metropolis: Chicago And The Great West*
Alfred W. Crosby's *The Columbian Exchange*
Hamid Dabashi's *Iran: A People Interrupted*
David Brion Davis's *The Problem of Slavery in the Age of Revolution*
Nathalie Zemon Davis's *The Return of Martin Guerre*
Jared Diamond's *Guns, Germs & Steel: the Fate of Human Societies*
Frank Dikotter's *Mao's Great Famine*
John W Dower's *War Without Mercy: Race And Power In The Pacific War*
W. E. B. Du Bois's *The Souls of Black Folk*
Richard J. Evans's *In Defence of History*
Lucien Febvre's *The Problem of Unbelief in the 16th Century*
Sheila Fitzpatrick's *Everyday Stalinism*

Eric Foner's *Reconstruction: America's Unfinished Revolution, 1863-1877*
Michel Foucault's *Discipline and Punish*
Michel Foucault's *History of Sexuality*
Francis Fukuyama's *The End of History and the Last Man*
John Lewis Gaddis's *We Now Know: Rethinking Cold War History*
Ernest Gellner's *Nations and Nationalism*
Eugene Genovese's *Roll, Jordan, Roll: The World the Slaves Made*
Carlo Ginzburg's *The Night Battles*
Daniel Goldhagen's *Hitler's Willing Executioners*
Jack Goldstone's *Revolution and Rebellion in the Early Modern World*
Antonio Gramsci's *The Prison Notebooks*
Alexander Hamilton, John Jay & James Madison's *The Federalist Papers*
Christopher Hill's *The World Turned Upside Down*
Carole Hillenbrand's *The Crusades: Islamic Perspectives*
Thomas Hobbes's *Leviathan*
Eric Hobsbawm's *The Age Of Revolution*
John A. Hobson's *Imperialism: A Study*
Albert Hourani's *History of the Arab Peoples*
Samuel P. Huntington's *The Clash of Civilizations and the Remaking of World Order*
C. L. R. James's *The Black Jacobins*
Tony Judt's *Postwar: A History of Europe Since 1945*
Ernst Kantorowicz's *The King's Two Bodies: A Study in Medieval Political Theology*
Paul Kennedy's *The Rise and Fall of the Great Powers*
Ian Kershaw's *The "Hitler Myth": Image and Reality in the Third Reich*
John Maynard Keynes's *The General Theory of Employment, Interest and Money*
Charles P. Kindleberger's *Manias, Panics and Crashes*
Martin Luther King Jr's *Why We Can't Wait*
Henry Kissinger's *World Order: Reflections on the Character of Nations and the Course of History*
Thomas Kuhn's *The Structure of Scientific Revolutions*
Georges Lefebvre's *The Coming of the French Revolution*
John Locke's *Two Treatises of Government*
Niccolò Machiavelli's *The Prince*
Thomas Robert Malthus's *An Essay on the Principle of Population*
Mahmood Mamdani's *Citizen and Subject: Contemporary Africa And The Legacy Of Late Colonialism*
Karl Marx's *Capital*
Stanley Milgram's *Obedience to Authority*
John Stuart Mill's *On Liberty*
Thomas Paine's *Common Sense*
Thomas Paine's *Rights of Man*
Geoffrey Parker's *Global Crisis: War, Climate Change and Catastrophe in the Seventeenth Century*
Jonathan Riley-Smith's *The First Crusade and the Idea of Crusading*
Jean-Jacques Rousseau's *The Social Contract*
Joan Wallach Scott's *Gender and the Politics of History*
Theda Skocpol's *States and Social Revolutions*
Adam Smith's *The Wealth of Nations*
Timothy Snyder's *Bloodlands: Europe Between Hitler and Stalin*
Sun Tzu's *The Art of War*
Keith Thomas's *Religion and the Decline of Magic*
Thucydides's *The History of the Peloponnesian War*
Frederick Jackson Turner's *The Significance of the Frontier in American History*
Odd Arne Westad's *The Global Cold War: Third World Interventions And The Making Of Our Times*

The Macat Library By Discipline

LITERATURE

Chinua Achebe's *An Image of Africa: Racism in Conrad's Heart of Darkness*
Roland Barthes's *Mythologies*
Homi K. Bhabha's *The Location of Culture*
Judith Butler's *Gender Trouble*
Simone De Beauvoir's *The Second Sex*
Ferdinand De Saussure's *Course in General Linguistics*
T. S. Eliot's *The Sacred Wood: Essays on Poetry and Criticism*
Zora Neale Huston's *Characteristics of Negro Expression*
Toni Morrison's *Playing in the Dark: Whiteness in the American Literary Imagination*
Edward Said's *Orientalism*
Gayatri Chakravorty Spivak's *Can the Subaltern Speak?*
Mary Wollstonecraft's *A Vindication of the Rights of Women*
Virginia Woolf's *A Room of One's Own*

PHILOSOPHY

Elizabeth Anscombe's *Modern Moral Philosophy*
Hannah Arendt's *The Human Condition*
Aristotle's *Metaphysics*
Aristotle's *Nicomachean Ethics*
Edmund Gettier's *Is Justified True Belief Knowledge?*
Georg Wilhelm Friedrich Hegel's *Phenomenology of Spirit*
David Hume's *Dialogues Concerning Natural Religion*
David Hume's *The Enquiry for Human Understanding*
Immanuel Kant's *Religion within the Boundaries of Mere Reason*
Immanuel Kant's *Critique of Pure Reason*
Søren Kierkegaard's *The Sickness Unto Death*
Søren Kierkegaard's *Fear and Trembling*
C. S. Lewis's *The Abolition of Man*
Alasdair MacIntyre's *After Virtue*
Marcus Aurelius's *Meditations*
Friedrich Nietzsche's *On the Genealogy of Morality*
Friedrich Nietzsche's *Beyond Good and Evil*
Plato's *Republic*
Plato's *Symposium*
Jean-Jacques Rousseau's *The Social Contract*
Gilbert Ryle's *The Concept of Mind*
Baruch Spinoza's *Ethics*
Sun Tzu's *The Art of War*
Ludwig Wittgenstein's *Philosophical Investigations*

POLITICS

Benedict Anderson's *Imagined Communities*
Aristotle's *Politics*
Bernard Bailyn's *The Ideological Origins of the American Revolution*
Edmund Burke's *Reflections on the Revolution in France*
John C. Calhoun's *A Disquisition on Government*
Ha-Joon Chang's *Kicking Away the Ladder*
Hamid Dabashi's *Iran: A People Interrupted*
Hamid Dabashi's *Theology of Discontent: The Ideological Foundation of the Islamic Revolution in Iran*
Robert Dahl's *Democracy and its Critics*
Robert Dahl's *Who Governs?*
David Brion Davis's *The Problem of Slavery in the Age of Revolution*

Alexis De Tocqueville's *Democracy in America*
James Ferguson's *The Anti-Politics Machine*
Frank Dikotter's *Mao's Great Famine*
Sheila Fitzpatrick's *Everyday Stalinism*
Eric Foner's *Reconstruction: America's Unfinished Revolution, 1863-1877*
Milton Friedman's *Capitalism and Freedom*
Francis Fukuyama's *The End of History and the Last Man*
John Lewis Gaddis's *We Now Know: Rethinking Cold War History*
Ernest Gellner's *Nations and Nationalism*
David Graeber's *Debt: the First 5000 Years*
Antonio Gramsci's *The Prison Notebooks*
Alexander Hamilton, John Jay & James Madison's *The Federalist Papers*
Friedrich Hayek's *The Road to Serfdom*
Christopher Hill's *The World Turned Upside Down*
Thomas Hobbes's *Leviathan*
John A. Hobson's *Imperialism: A Study*
Samuel P. Huntington's *The Clash of Civilizations and the Remaking of World Order*
Tony Judt's *Postwar: A History of Europe Since 1945*
David C. Kang's *China Rising: Peace, Power and Order in East Asia*
Paul Kennedy's *The Rise and Fall of Great Powers*
Robert Keohane's *After Hegemony*
Martin Luther King Jr.'s *Why We Can't Wait*
Henry Kissinger's *World Order: Reflections on the Character of Nations and the Course of History*
John Locke's *Two Treatises of Government*
Niccolò Machiavelli's *The Prince*
Thomas Robert Malthus's *An Essay on the Principle of Population*
Mahmood Mamdani's *Citizen and Subject: Contemporary Africa And The Legacy Of Late Colonialism*
Karl Marx's *Capital*
John Stuart Mill's *On Liberty*
John Stuart Mill's *Utilitarianism*
Hans Morgenthau's *Politics Among Nations*
Thomas Paine's *Common Sense*
Thomas Paine's *Rights of Man*
Thomas Piketty's *Capital in the Twenty-First Century*
Robert D. Putman's *Bowling Alone*
John Rawls's *Theory of Justice*
Jean-Jacques Rousseau's *The Social Contract*
Theda Skocpol's *States and Social Revolutions*
Adam Smith's *The Wealth of Nations*
Sun Tzu's *The Art of War*
Henry David Thoreau's *Civil Disobedience*
Thucydides's *The History of the Peloponnesian War*
Kenneth Waltz's *Theory of International Politics*
Max Weber's *Politics as a Vocation*
Odd Arne Westad's *The Global Cold War: Third World Interventions And The Making Of Our Times*

POSTCOLONIAL STUDIES

Roland Barthes's *Mythologies*
Frantz Fanon's *Black Skin, White Masks*
Homi K. Bhabha's *The Location of Culture*
Gustavo Gutiérrez's *A Theology of Liberation*
Edward Said's *Orientalism*
Gayatri Chakravorty Spivak's *Can the Subaltern Speak?*

The Macat Library By Discipline

PSYCHOLOGY

Gordon Allport's *The Nature of Prejudice*
Alan Baddeley & Graham Hitch's *Aggression: A Social Learning Analysis*
Albert Bandura's *Aggression: A Social Learning Analysis*
Leon Festinger's *A Theory of Cognitive Dissonance*
Sigmund Freud's *The Interpretation of Dreams*
Betty Friedan's *The Feminine Mystique*
Michael R. Gottfredson & Travis Hirschi's *A General Theory of Crime*
Eric Hoffer's *The True Believer: Thoughts on the Nature of Mass Movements*
William James's *Principles of Psychology*
Elizabeth Loftus's *Eyewitness Testimony*
A. H. Maslow's *A Theory of Human Motivation*
Stanley Milgram's *Obedience to Authority*
Steven Pinker's *The Better Angels of Our Nature*
Oliver Sacks's *The Man Who Mistook His Wife For a Hat*
Richard Thaler & Cass Sunstein's *Nudge: Improving Decisions About Health, Wealth and Happiness*
Amos Tversky's *Judgment under Uncertainty: Heuristics and Biases*
Philip Zimbardo's *The Lucifer Effect*

SCIENCE

Rachel Carson's *Silent Spring*
William Cronon's *Nature's Metropolis: Chicago And The Great West*
Alfred W. Crosby's *The Columbian Exchange*
Charles Darwin's *On the Origin of Species*
Richard Dawkin's *The Selfish Gene*
Thomas Kuhn's *The Structure of Scientific Revolutions*
Geoffrey Parker's *Global Crisis: War, Climate Change and Catastrophe in the Seventeenth Century*
Mathis Wackernagel & William Rees's *Our Ecological Footprint*

SOCIOLOGY

Michelle Alexander's *The New Jim Crow: Mass Incarceration in the Age of Colorblindness*
Gordon Allport's *The Nature of Prejudice*
Albert Bandura's *Aggression: A Social Learning Analysis*
Hanna Batatu's *The Old Social Classes And The Revolutionary Movements Of Iraq*
Ha-Joon Chang's *Kicking Away the Ladder*
W. E. B. Du Bois's *The Souls of Black Folk*
Émile Durkheim's *On Suicide*
Frantz Fanon's *Black Skin, White Masks*
Frantz Fanon's *The Wretched of the Earth*
Eric Foner's *Reconstruction: America's Unfinished Revolution, 1863-1877*
Eugene Genovese's *Roll, Jordan, Roll: The World the Slaves Made*
Jack Goldstone's *Revolution and Rebellion in the Early Modern World*
Antonio Gramsci's *The Prison Notebooks*
Richard Herrnstein & Charles A Murray's *The Bell Curve: Intelligence and Class Structure in American Life*
Eric Hoffer's *The True Believer: Thoughts on the Nature of Mass Movements*
Jane Jacobs's *The Death and Life of Great American Cities*
Robert Lucas's *Why Doesn't Capital Flow from Rich to Poor Countries?*
Jay Macleod's *Ain't No Makin' It: Aspirations and Attainment in a Low Income Neighborhood*
Elaine May's *Homeward Bound: American Families in the Cold War Era*
Douglas McGregor's *The Human Side of Enterprise*
C. Wright Mills's *The Sociological Imagination*

Thomas Piketty's *Capital in the Twenty-First Century*
Robert D. Putman's *Bowling Alone*
David Riesman's *The Lonely Crowd: A Study of the Changing American Character*
Edward Said's *Orientalism*
Joan Wallach Scott's *Gender and the Politics of History*
Theda Skocpol's *States and Social Revolutions*
Max Weber's *The Protestant Ethic and the Spirit of Capitalism*

THEOLOGY

Augustine's *Confessions*
Benedict's *Rule of St Benedict*
Gustavo Gutiérrez's *A Theology of Liberation*
Carole Hillenbrand's *The Crusades: Islamic Perspectives*
David Hume's *Dialogues Concerning Natural Religion*
Immanuel Kant's *Religion within the Boundaries of Mere Reason*
Ernst Kantorowicz's *The King's Two Bodies: A Study in Medieval Political Theology*
Søren Kierkegaard's *The Sickness Unto Death*
C. S. Lewis's *The Abolition of Man*
Saba Mahmood's *The Politics of Piety: The Islamic Revival and the Feminist Subjec*t
Baruch Spinoza's *Ethics*
Keith Thomas's *Religion and the Decline of Magic*

COMING SOON

Chris Argyris's *The Individual and the Organisation*
Seyla Benhabib's *The Rights of Others*
Walter Benjamin's *The Work Of Art in the Age of Mechanical Reproduction*
John Berger's *Ways of Seeing*
Pierre Bourdieu's *Outline of a Theory of Practice*
Mary Douglas's *Purity and Danger*
Roland Dworkin's *Taking Rights Seriously*
James G. March's *Exploration and Exploitation in Organisational Learning*
Ikujiro Nonaka's *A Dynamic Theory of Organizational Knowledge Creation*
Griselda Pollock's *Vision and Difference*
Amartya Sen's *Inequality Re-Examined*
Susan Sontag's *On Photography*
Yasser Tabbaa's *The Transformation of Islamic Art*
Ludwig von Mises's *Theory of Money and Credit*

Macat Disciplines

Access the greatest ideas and thinkers across entire disciplines, including

AFRICANA STUDIES

Chinua Achebe's *An Image of Africa: Racism in Conrad's Heart of Darkness*

W. E. B. Du Bois's *The Souls of Black Folk*

Zora Neale Hurston's *Characteristics of Negro Expression*

Martin Luther King Jr.'s *Why We Can't Wait*

Toni Morrison's *Playing in the Dark: Whiteness in the American Literary Imagination*

Macat analyses are available from all good bookshops and libraries.

Access hundreds of analyses through one, multimedia tool.

Join free for one month libra   macat.com

Macat Disciplines

Access the greatest ideas and thinkers across entire disciplines, including

FEMINISM, GENDER AND QUEER STUDIES

Simone De Beauvoir's
The Second Sex

Michel Foucault's
History of Sexuality

Betty Friedan's
The Feminine Mystique

Saba Mahmood's
*The Politics of Piety:
The Islamic Revival and
the Feminist Subject*

Joan Wallach Scott's
*Gender and the
Politics of History*

Mary Wollstonecraft's
*A Vindication of the
Rights of Woman*

Virginia Woolf's
A Room of One's Own

Judith Butler's
Gender Trouble

 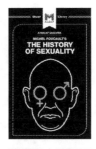  

Macat Disciplines

Access the greatest ideas and thinkers across entire disciplines, including

INEQUALITY

Ha-Joon Chang's, *Kicking Away the Ladder*

David Graeber's, *Debt: The First 5000 Years*

Robert E. Lucas's, *Why Doesn't Capital Flow from Rich To Poor Countries?*

Thomas Piketty's, *Capital in the Twenty-First Century*

Amartya Sen's, *Inequality Re-Examined*

Mahbub Ul Haq's, *Reflections on Human Development*

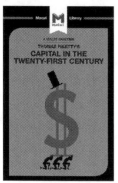

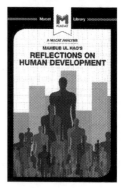

Macat analyses are available from all good bookshops and libraries.

Access hundreds of analyses through one, multimedia tool.
Join free for one month **library.macat.com**

Macat Disciplines

Access the greatest ideas and thinkers across entire disciplines, including

CRIMINOLOGY

Michelle Alexander's
*The New Jim Crow:
Mass Incarceration in the
Age of Colorblindness*

**Michael R. Gottfredson
& Travis Hirschi's**
A General Theory of Crime

Elizabeth Loftus's
Eyewitness Testimony

**Richard Herrnstein
& Charles A. Murray's**
*The Bell Curve: Intelligence and
Class Structure in American Life*

Jay Macleod's
*Ain't No Makin' It:
Aspirations and Attainment in a
Low-Income Neighborhood*

Philip Zimbardo's
The Lucifer Effect

Macat Disciplines

Access the greatest ideas and thinkers across entire disciplines, including

Postcolonial Studies

Roland Barthes's *Mythologies*
Frantz Fanon's *Black Skin, White Masks*
Homi K. Bhabha's *The Location of Culture*
Gustavo Gutiérrez's *A Theology of Liberation*
Edward Said's *Orientalism*
Gayatri Chakravorty Spivak's *Can the Subaltern Speak?*

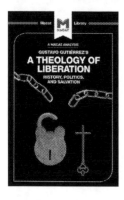
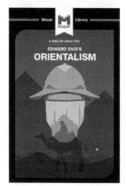

Macat analyses are available from all good bookshops and libraries.

Access hundreds of analyses through one, multimedia tool.
Join free for one month **library.macat.com**

Macat Disciplines

Access the greatest ideas and thinkers across entire disciplines, including

GLOBALIZATION

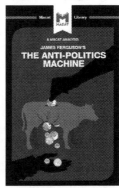

Arjun Appadurai's, *Modernity at Large: Cultural Dimensions of Globalisation*

James Ferguson's, *The Anti-Politics Machine*

Geert Hofstede's, *Culture's Consequences*

Amartya Sen's, *Development as Freedom*

Macat analyses are available from all good bookshops and libraries.

Access hundreds of analyses through one, multimedia tool. Join free for one month **library.macat.com**

Macat Pairs

Analyse historical and modern issues from opposite sides of an argument. Pairs include:

HOW TO RUN AN ECONOMY

John Maynard Keynes's
The General Theory OF Employment, Interest and Money

Classical economics suggests that market economies are self-correcting in times of recession or depression, and tend toward full employment and output. But English economist John Maynard Keynes disagrees.

In his ground-breaking 1936 study *The General Theory*, Keynes argues that traditional economics has misunderstood the causes of unemployment. Employment is not determined by the price of labor; it is directly linked to demand. Keynes believes market economies are by nature unstable, and so require government intervention. Spurred on by the social catastrophe of the Great Depression of the 1930s, he sets out to revolutionize the way the world thinks

Milton Friedman's
The Role of Monetary Policy

Friedman's 1968 paper changed the course of economic theory. In just 17 pages, he demolished existing theory and outlined an effective alternate monetary policy designed to secure 'high employment, stable prices and rapid growth.'

Friedman demonstrated that monetary policy plays a vital role in broader economic stability and argued that economists got their monetary policy wrong in the 1950s and 1960s by misunderstanding the relationship between inflation and unemployment. Previous generations of economists had believed that governments could permanently decrease unemployment by permitting inflation—and vice versa. Friedman's most original contribution was to show that this supposed trade-off is an illusion that only works in the short term.

Macat Disciplines

Access the greatest ideas and thinkers across entire disciplines, including

THE FUTURE OF DEMOCRACY

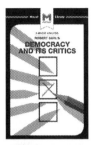

Robert A. Dahl's, *Democracy and Its Critics*
Robert A. Dahl's, *Who Governs?*
Alexis De Toqueville's, *Democracy in America*
Niccolò Machiavelli's, *The Prince*
John Stuart Mill's, *On Liberty*
Robert D. Putnam's, *Bowling Alone*
Jean-Jacques Rousseau's, *The Social Contract*
Henry David Thoreau's, *Civil Disobedience*

Macat Disciplines

Access the greatest ideas and thinkers across entire disciplines, including

TOTALITARIANISM

Sheila Fitzpatrick's, *Everyday Stalinism*
Ian Kershaw's, *The "Hitler Myth"*
Timothy Snyder's, *Bloodlands*

Macat analyses are available from all good bookshops and libraries.

Access hundreds of analyses through one, multimedia tool.
Join free for one month **library.macat.com**

Macat Pairs

Analyse historical and modern issues from opposite sides of an argument. Pairs include:

RACE AND IDENTITY

Zora Neale Hurston's
Characteristics of Negro Expression

Using material collected on anthropological expeditions to the South, Zora Neale Hurston explains how expression in African American culture in the early twentieth century departs from the art of white America. At the time, African American art was often criticized for copying white culture. For Hurston, this criticism misunderstood how art works. European tradition views art as something fixed. But Hurston describes a creative process that is alive, ever-changing, and largely improvisational. She maintains that African American art works through a process called 'mimicry'—where an imitated object or verbal pattern, for example, is reshaped and altered until it becomes something new, novel—and worthy of attention.

Frantz Fanon's
Black Skin, White Masks

Black Skin, White Masks offers a radical analysis of the psychological effects of colonization on the colonized.

Fanon witnessed the effects of colonization first hand both in his birthplace, Martinique, and again later in life when he worked as a psychiatrist in another French colony, Algeria. His text is uncompromising in form and argument. He dissects the dehumanizing effects of colonialism, arguing that it destroys the native sense of identity, forcing people to adapt to an alien set of values—including a core belief that they are inferior. This results in deep psychological trauma.

Fanon's work played a pivotal role in the civil rights movements of the 1960s.

Macat analyses are available from all good bookshops and libraries.

Access hundreds of analyses through one, multimedia tool.
Join free for one month **library.macat.com**

Macat Pairs

Analyse historical and modern issues from opposite sides of an argument. Pairs include:

INTERNATIONAL RELATIONS IN THE 21ST CENTURY

Samuel P. Huntington's
The Clash of Civilisations

In his highly influential 1996 book, Huntington offers a vision of a post-Cold War world in which conflict takes place not between competing ideologies but between cultures. The worst clash, he argues, will be between the Islamic world and the West: the West's arrogance and belief that its culture is a "gift" to the world will come into conflict with Islam's obstinacy and concern that its culture is under attack from a morally decadent "other."

Clash inspired much debate between different political schools of thought. But its greatest impact came in helping define American foreign policy in the wake of the 2001 terrorist attacks in New York and Washington.

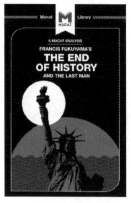

Francis Fukuyama's
The End of History and the Last Man

Published in 1992, *The End of History and the Last Man* argues that capitalist democracy is the final destination for all societies. Fukuyama believed democracy triumphed during the Cold War because it lacks the "fundamental contradictions" inherent in communism and satisfies our yearning for freedom and equality. Democracy therefore marks the endpoint in the evolution of ideology, and so the "end of history." There will still be "events," but no fundamental change in ideology.

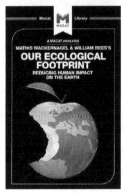

Macat Pairs

Analyse historical and modern issues from opposite sides of an argument. Pairs include:

ARE WE FUNDAMENTALLY GOOD - OR BAD?

Steven Pinker's
The Better Angels of Our Nature

Stephen Pinker's gloriously optimistic 2011 book argues that, despite humanity's biological tendency toward violence, we are, in fact, less violent today than ever before. To prove his case, Pinker lays out pages of detailed statistical evidence. For him, much of the credit for the decline goes to the eighteenth-century Enlightenment movement, whose ideas of liberty, tolerance, and respect for the value of human life filtered down through society and affected how people thought. That psychological change led to behavioral change—and overall we became more peaceful. Critics countered that humanity could never overcome the biological urge toward violence; others argued that Pinker's statistics were flawed.

Philip Zimbardo's
The Lucifer Effect

Some psychologists believe those who commit cruelty are innately evil. Zimbardo disagrees. In *The Lucifer Effect*, he argues that sometimes good people do evil things simply because of the situations they find themselves in, citing many historical examples to illustrate his point. Zimbardo details his 1971 Stanford prison experiment, where ordinary volunteers playing guards in a mock prison rapidly became abusive. But he also describes the tortures committed by US army personnel in Iraq's Abu Ghraib prison in 2003—and how he himself testified in defence of one of those guards. committed by US army personnel in Iraq's Abu Ghraib prison in 2003—and how he himself testified in defence of one of those guards.

Macat analyses are available from all good bookshops and libraries.

Access hundreds of analyses through one, multimedia tool.

Join free for one month **library.macat.com**

Macat Pairs

Analyse historical and modern issues from opposite sides of an argument. Pairs include:

HOW WE RELATE TO EACH OTHER AND SOCIETY

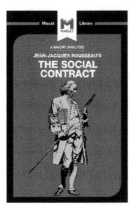

Jean-Jacques Rousseau's
The Social Contract

Rousseau's famous work sets out the radical concept of the 'social contract': a give-and-take relationship between individual freedom and social order.

If people are free to do as they like, governed only by their own sense of justice, they are also vulnerable to chaos and violence. To avoid this, Rousseau proposes, they should agree to give up some freedom to benefit from the protection of social and political organization. But this deal is only just if societies are led by the collective needs and desires of the people, and able to control the private interests of individuals. For Rousseau, the only legitimate form of government is rule by the people.

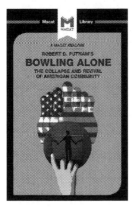

Robert D. Putnam's
Bowling Alone

In *Bowling Alone*, Robert Putnam argues that Americans have become disconnected from one another and from the institutions of their common life, and investigates the consequences of this change.

Looking at a range of indicators, from membership in formal organizations to the number of invitations being extended to informal dinner parties, Putnam demonstrates that Americans are interacting less and creating less "social capital" – with potentially disastrous implications for their society.

It would be difficult to overstate the impact of *Bowling Alone*, one of the most frequently cited social science publications of the last half-century.

Macat analyses are available from all good bookshops and libraries.

Access hundreds of analyses through one, multimedia tool.
Join free for one month **library.macat.com**

Printed in the United States
by Baker & Taylor Publisher Services